Colour Beyond the Surface: Art in Architecture

Fiona McLachlan

LUND
HUMPHRIES

First published in 2022 by Lund Humphries

Lund Humphries
Huckletree Shoreditch
Alphabeta Building
18 Finsbury Square
London, EC2A 1AH
UK

www.lundhumphries.com

Colour Beyond the Surface: Art in Architecture

ISBN: 978–1–84822–570–1

A Cataloguing-in-Publication record for this book is
available from the British Library.

Front cover: Antoni Malinowski/Haworth Tompkins,
stair at Donmar Warehouse, London, 2014. Detail of a
photograph by Valerie Bennett.

Copy edited by Pamela Bertram
Designed by Jacqui Cornish
Proofread by Patrick Cole
Cover designed by Paul Arnot
Set in Circular Std and Sofia Pro
Printed in Estonia

Contents

0.1　Derek Roberts, *Study: Untitled (2)*, oil on canvas, December 1994–July 1996, 81 × 71 cm (31 ⅞ × 27 ¹⁵⁄₁₆ in)

Preface

A few years ago, following a public lecture on colour and wellbeing, a subject I had previously avoided, I was invited to make a colour design installation in a hospital dementia ward. A further two projects have followed and, in each case, the physical act of making the installation allowed time to think, time to observe – as each colour shifted the appearance of its neighbours – and time to meet the users. There were, of course, a few doubters, but the majority expressed overwhelmingly positive reactions as the colour transformed the spaces. The wall paintings lie somewhere between art and architecture. They were a way of applying colour, not in a decorative manner, but in an affective way, and became the starting point for this book.

A painting by the artist Derek Roberts hangs in my hall (fig.0.1). A photograph cannot capture the thickness of one layer of oil paint laid over another, the erratic brush marks revealing one colour peeking out through another between the gaps in the strokes. More than anything, the painting speaks of the time Derek sat, unsatisfied, in his sheepskin-lined wicker chair looking, then overpainting and sitting and looking again, then slowly reaching a point of contentment over a prolonged period. Each layer of colour is evident as a palimpsest, the mark of an earlier form, now overpainted, which is visible only as an undulation on the surface.

As an architect, educator and colour researcher, I have now spent many years learning, teaching and experimenting with colour in architectural design. Artists, particularly painters, work with colour every day. Educationally, our disciplines have drifted apart. This book aims to bridge between the practices of art and architecture, taking colour as a focus and potential common ground.

Acknowledgements

With thanks to the University of Edinburgh/
Edinburgh College of Art for research funding
and a semester of sabbatical, which allowed
time to collate my notes and thoughts, and write
intensively; to my supportive and stimulating
colleagues in the Edinburgh School of Architecture
and Landscape Architecture (ESALA), my academic
home for over 30 years. To Val Rose, commissioning
editor at Lund Humphries, for her enthusiastic
support for the book. Particular thanks to Professor
Iain Boyd Whyte for his sharp-eyed edits to hone
the text, and to all the artists and architects who
willingly gave their time to be interviewed and for
their permission to include their work. Finally, to
my son Max and husband Ewen for reading the first
draft, and for contributions of photographs and
myriad skills in digital image manipulation.

0.2 and 0.3   Fiona McLachlan, *Autumn*, eggshell on emulsion, Royal Edinburgh Hospital, 2019

1 Introduction: Spatial Synchronicity

A painting made on canvas in a studio setting and conventionally exhibited within a gallery space invites the audience to study its composition, meaning and production. It carries with it a concept of its audience, as the object of the fixed gaze of the viewer, albeit a momentary focus in a generally unpredictable setting. Size is significant, with very large canvases taking on more of the characteristics of a mural. An artwork embedded in an architectural surface will become an integral part of the space, an essential component of the fabric and atmosphere, and glimpsed in the peripheral vision of an often inattentive, moving audience. It is also subject to a different set of vulnerabilities than a peripatetic canvas.

In making his wall painting, *The Stairwell Project* (fig.1.1), at the Scottish National Gallery of Modern Art in Edinburgh (2010), the artist Richard Wright allowed himself to be 'deflected by the architecture'.[1] The initial conceptual view of the work was altered by the act of installation in which the work drifted over the vaulted ceiling. At Greenwich (2016), Wright made a further installation in the Great Hall of the Queen's House (by Inigo Jones), which wraps the ceiling and upper walls with a delicate gold leaf pattern. Both works became synchronous with the idiosyncrasies of surface and form, while at the same time, Wright's inscriptions modified the reading of architectural surface and space. In these examples, the artist was working in existing buildings, so there was no dialogue with an architect, only with the architectural surfaces. The presence of the artwork adds a further layer of meaning that may not be immediately apparent. We may be challenged by its presence, made momentarily curious and observant.

Historically, there was little separation between art and architecture, and an expectation that architectural surfaces would be decorated. The temples of Greek antiquity were brightly painted; Raphael and Michelangelo were both painters and architects. For many, the Baroque period exemplifies the intertwining of visual art, sculpture and architecture. Today, the physical demands of making art within an architectural space, the economic context of portable art as commodity, and the demands of the contemporary building industry have all contributed to a decline in such permanent installations, and the disciplines have drifted apart. Yet, there are examples of successful collaborations where a symbiotic relationship between art and architecture is firmly established, to the point where art and architecture work inseparably as a *Gesamtkunstwerk* – a 'total work of art'. How do artists and architects negotiate their different approaches? How does the artwork affect our experience of architectural space?

Colour, although often conceived of as a decorative afterthought, fundamentally affects our spatial and temporal experience of space, yet many architects will admit to a nervousness when working with colour. Although we are now seeing a renewed interest, sadly, it is often used poorly, with no strategic purpose and constrained by confusion and dogma. As colour is complex and frequently misunderstood, the reader will be introduced to colour as an ambiguous, transient phenomenon that can contribute to multiple readings of material surface and space. At the scale of architecture, which is experienced in perspective and through the moving body, the effect of colour on the senses is amplified, and has long been considered as a danger to form by introducing a competitive experiential element. While architects work with colour vicariously, artists – and particularly painters – confront nuanced decisions on colour each day. These in turn will

directly affect the spatial reading and interpretation of their work. In her compendium handbook on the philosophy of colour, the contemporary philosopher Fiona Macpherson reflects that artists have for centuries studied and replicated unusual chromatic experiences that continue to puzzle psychologists and neuroscientists. She points out, for example, that while a blueish-yellow is an impossible concept, an artist may skilfully mimic the experience of a graduated sky drifting upwards from yellow to blue using moderated grey tones at the point of intersection, but without ever becoming green.[2] Simultaneously simple, yet complex as a metaphysical experience, apparently unnecessary, yet profoundly affective, the appearance of colour varies constantly with light conditions and is entirely contingent on the context and reflectance of the material surface as well as the social, cultural and physiological attributes of the viewer.

This book aims to highlight transactions between art and architecture, providing insights from both perspectives, using historical examples to establish significant themes. It will focus on examples where the artwork is embedded as a permanent installation, and where art and architecture become intertwined in the holistic experience and appreciation of architectural space.

The book is structured in three parts, encompassing architecture, art and collaborative practices. The first part begins with a discussion of architectural surfaces as a locus for artwork and the potential tensions that can arise, both positive and negative. As with Richard Wright's surface scripting, Alan Johnston's subtle monochrome wall drawing at the Tate Gallery in London, discussed in Chapter 2, offers a different reading, reinforcing and intensifying the existing architectural form. Other examples, such as Theo van Doesburg's installation at the Café Aubette in Strasbourg, clash and disrupt the form and surface with colour and geometry. Tensions often help to make art and architecture more engaging, forcing us to see the familiar in an unfamiliar way. Chapter 3 considers polychromy and its application by a series of architects, who draw on their own artistic practice to develop a skill and facility with colour, preferring to stay in control of the articulation of form and composition.

In Part II, principles of art practice that are significant to spatial perception are considered.

Chapter 4 investigates the evolving concept of pictorial space, of depth alluded to within an image, and how this might extend beyond the surface of an artwork to affect the experience of space through light and colour. Juhani Pallasmaa suggests that architecture is the domain of peripheral vision.[3] We absorb, then assimilate, our surroundings in an absent-minded condition of familiarity. As we move through architectural space, our visual and bodily awareness – our proprioceptive experiences – become intertwined. Our viewpoint constantly shifts as the body moves and the eyes' saccadic movements dart from figure to ground, from fragment to form, from edge to edge, from light to dark, from one colour to another, making sense of our surroundings to navigate. Material surfaces are therefore fundamental to architecture. Varying in appearance in light and shadow, they can provide an artist with an extended field, but will also place restrictions. The technology of production will vary with the material surface, the tools and pigments available, and the need for durability. Chapter 5 focuses on the contribution of artwork to architecture through a wide range of material and immaterial practices.

The artist Fernand Léger referred to his wall paintings deferentially as 'peinture d'ameublement', alluding to a musician who refers to his music as furniture music – 'heard rather than listened to'.[4] Chapter 6 introduces the perspective of the artist, drawing on a series of interviews with contemporary artists working predominately in the UK. How do they feel about their work being experienced in the periphery of vision? How does their material palette alter, knowing that the work will be vulnerable to the conditions of its setting? How do they understand pictorial space in relation to their own work and how it might contribute to the experience of the architectural setting?

The final part of the book considers how artists and architects collaborate. In some cases, as discussed in Chapter 7, the artist may become a sounding board to challenge and to inject a different perspective, as was the case between Rémy Zaugg and the Swiss architects Jacques Herzog and Pierre de Meuron. Some works may become interlaced into the fabric of architecture, demanding an intense relationship between the

LEFT

1.1   Richard Wright, *The Stairwell Project*, 2010, acrylic on plastered wall/ceiling, Scottish National Gallery of Modern Art (Modern Two) Edinburgh

parties, as between Eric Parry Architects and the sculptor Richard Deacon. Often an architect may take the lead, as is demonstrated at the Ciudad Universitaria de Caracas, Venezuela in the 1950s by Carlos Raúl Villanueva. A collaboration may be a one-off or instead lead to a longstanding dialogue, for example, between contemporary architects Haworth Tompkins and the artist Antoni Malinowski, whose work forms a thread through several chapters and illustrates the significance of colour, light, spatial and material practice. Collaborations can be complex; artists must learn skills and navigate through logistical processes that are inherent to architecture, and architects and clients may need to take a leap of faith in accepting an unpredictable outcome. How do professional commissioners contribute to these interactions as an intermediary, matching clients to artists and architects? What lessons have been learnt that makes a collaboration successful?

The final chapter celebrates the exuberant and eclectic project commissioned by Alain de Botton for Living Architecture – *A House for Essex* by artist Grayson Perry and FAT Architecture, which integrates art and architecture as both symbiotic and synchronous.

PART I
THE ARCHITECTURE

2 Surface Tensions

The simple, vaulted rectangular form of the Scrovegni (Arena) Chapel in Padua (1303–5) is elevated to a place of extraordinary beauty by Giotto's frescoes and most dramatically by the deep azure blue of the ceiling (fig.2.1). Figurative panels are structured and ordered between painted architectural elements, which – while flat – give an illusion of relief. Although at one level this is entirely surface decoration, the colour and formal constructions are deeply affective on the human experience of the architectural volume. In her book *Painting: Mysteries and Confessions*, the artist Tess Jaray describes her fascination with the 'balanced equilibrium' between the paintings and the architecture and the 'unfathomable depth' of the 'sky'.[1] For Jaray, this dynamic tension is arresting yet coherent. The eye and mind are confronted with a simultaneous effect of surface combined with real and illusory volume.

In architecture, the idea of surface has become contested and somewhat confused. This was in part due to the development of frame constructions, the separation of structure and skin, the suspension of the need for solid walls and the desire for apparently unrestrained space flowing freely from inside to outside. Architecture as a profession developed in Europe around the 16th century, emerging from the craft skills of master masons and draughtsmen, yet until the early 19th century there was little separation between the visual arts. It was entirely acceptable for surfaces – particularly plaster or stucco surfaces in public buildings and homes – to be painted and decorated with colour and articulated through figurative and decorative paintings often made directly onto the walls and ceilings. Since the early 20th century, the arts have diverged, and with this parting, different conceptual thinking has become ingrained. In *Surface Architecture*, David Leatherbarrow and Mohsen Mostafavi discuss these uneasy relationships: 'deprived of ornament, and of load-bearing requirements, walling became "infill", a covering, container, or wrapper, hung behind, or in front of the open spaces of the frame. The status of walling as "image" was thus redefined'.[2] For the contemporary architect, the concept of surface as something apart from a formal enclosure can be intellectually problematic. Trained to consider the primacy of form and volume over surface, treatments of materials that alter appearance or texture, or impart narrative meaning, may be troubling. Consider Joseph Amato's observation: 'Surfaces are nature's instructors . . . They declare what is light and shadowy, near and far, what is at hand and imminent and what is remote in space and time. Beyond the forms and patterns they present, they offer the most immediate classifications and also the first clues to what is within things.'[3]

Human skin, while essential to life, is also thought of as wrapping, dressing and enclosing the more fundamental flesh, organs and bones. Surface and skin invite a sensual connection, an opacity that invites touch, exploration and discovery. Beauty that is merely 'skin deep' may be initially arresting, but ultimately considered as disappointingly shallow. The definition of surface, when characterised as a thin layer, is subservient to form and is quintessentially superficial. Yet surfaces contain and form the boundaries to three-dimensional space. James J. Gibson offers a contrasting position: 'why, in the triad of medium, substances and surfaces are surfaces so important? The surface is where most of the action is.'[4] Surfaces are revealed by the play of light. Their distinct light-reflective qualities at a microscopic material scale give rise to the colour we see. Surface decoration, including an applied layer of paint, may subvert or support form. Little has changed in the dialogue between artists and architects since the early 20th century, despite radical changes in architectural procurement, representation, means of production and the ability

2.1   Scrovegni Chapel, Padua, 1303–5, 2100 × 800 cm (826 ¾ × 314 ⅝ in); frescoes by Giotto

2.2   Fernand Léger, Study for mosaic mural at the University of Caracas, 1952 (Architect Carlos
Raúl Villanueva, 1944–7), gouache and India ink on paper, 30 × 89.5 cm (11 ¹³⁄₁₆ × 35 ¼ in)

to visualise and create complex three-dimensional space through computer-aided design (CAD) and virtual reality. A wall may wrap to become ceiling, fold and twist, but the essence of the relationships between form and surface remains. Form and surface therefore – although inseparable – may produce dissonance or resonance and the relationships between surface–edge–boundary and readings of form can be seen as unstable and open to interpretation.

For the easel painter, the surface is the extent of the work, the edges of the canvas are the boundaries and the skill is in making an illusion of form and space on the flat surface purely through the application, juxtaposition and scale of brushloads of paint. The surface of the canvas gives a very basic formal constraint for an artist painter. In a Walter Benjamin essay from 1915, a dialogue takes place between 'Margarethe' and a painter friend, 'Georg'. The artist explains that painting can never represent the radiant, phantasy colours she has experienced in a dream. Painting, the text suggests, does not begin with colour, but 'from the spiritual and the creative, from form', and concludes 'that the surface and not colour is the essence of painting'.[5] Walls and ceilings within architecture offer the artist surfaces at a vast scale in comparison to the easel canvas. These surfaces provided the earliest known sites for artistic expression through cave paintings. In 1934, the Bauhaus artist Willi

Baumeister noted: 'the surface is the primordial means, the first elementary medium of painting'.[6]

In a 1937 essay, the painter Fernand Léger (1881–1955) defined three categories of artistic activity – easel painting, decorative art and mural art – each with a very different audience and purpose.[7] Easel paintings are distinct because of their mobility and the off-site location of their production. The audience is conditioned to view easel paintings with a fixed and attentive gaze; they offer a window into another state, whether framed or not. Decorative art tends to be associated with objects or crafted surface, but distinctions between fine art and decorative art have since become blurred. Decorative art can personalise space, provide distinction, colour, texture and interest, but may have less autonomous meaning than an easel painting. According to Léger, a wall painting or mural is essentially different to the other two artforms as it must respond to its setting and architectural context to connect with both the physical form and the environmental conditions. The wall, floor or ceiling are not always flat; they are an inscribed landscape in which there will be obstacles, undulations, corners, doors and windows, constant variations in the light quality, and multiple viewpoints from which the surfaces are observed.

Wall and ceiling painting within architecture has declined since the 1950s to the extent that contemporary artists are rarely invited, or rarely involve themselves, in a direct relationship with architectural surfaces, with the exception of street artists. Art is commissioned or, more commonly, subsequently added to spaces with or without a specific resonance with the architectural context. Paradoxically, however, interest in spatial art is on the increase, with architecture providing the context and indeed eliciting a conversation between the art and the architectural site. Many such reactive and responsive examples are temporary, as Giuliana Bruno suggests: 'A widespread phenomenon is taking place in contemporary art as the mediatic configurations of art and architecture come closer together, converging in surface tension as they partake of common material ground. Art is melting into spatial construction, and as a consequence, architecture has become one of the most influential forms of imaging.'[8]

Spatial art heightens the experience of the architecture and demands attention in a similar way to a gallery exhibition. But art that is essentially a temporary, three-dimensional installation is therefore distinct again from Léger's definition of

mural art and very different from the easel painting. This chapter will consider the distinctive nature of architectural surfaces as a site for artwork that is intended to be 'permanent' – the interrelationships of form, scale and orientation, the vulnerability of surfaces through long-term use, and the logistical challenges of the site context.

FORM AND SURFACE – RESONANCE

At the Tate Britain in London, the artist Alan Johnston (b. 1945) was commissioned to inscribe the surfaces of a vaulted cafe space with a hand drawing, *Tactile Geometry* (2013), as part of the renovations by architects Caruso St John (fig.2.3). The pencil markings are meticulously conceived to draw attention to light and shadow. There is no colour, other than through a tonal shift in grey scale made by the multitude of tiny lines. The hand drawing was made with a team of eight assistants over a two-week period.[9] There is precision but also a looseness that makes the work sit gently on the surface. As a barely perceptible shadow drawing, it is an exceptionally subtle response

2.3   Alan Johnston, *Tactile Geometry*, 2013, pencil drawing on the vaulted ceiling of the Djanogly Café, Tate Britain, London

that reveals and accentuates the architectural form in a symbiotic manner. Many of the most enduring and spectacular examples of frescoes adorn the surfaces of ceilings and vaults. By contrast, contemporary architecture tends to either underplay the potential of ceilings, or to allow them to become peppered by poorly considered light fittings, extract grilles, smoke detectors, sprinklers and similar. These are the most neglected surfaces in contemporary architecture.

Historically, ceilings provided a canvas for artists to explore perspective, including a deliberately distorted perspective to evoke concepts of infinite space, for example, the Baroque collaboration between the artist Giovanni Battista Tiepolo and architect Balthasar Neumann at the Residenz, Würzburg (1751–3). Tiepolo had been working in the building for several years before the commission for the immense ceiling above the main staircase (fig.2.4). In their book, *Tiepolo and the Pictorial Intelligence*, Svetlana Alpers and Michael Baxendall make a detailed analysis of the development of the painting, its perspectival relationship to the moving viewer, and the subsequent modifications to the windows that mean we now see the painting literally in a different light from when it was completed.[10] In one section of the book, the authors draw attention to Tiepolo's unusual approach to composition in his easel paintings. For example, he might place figures to one side of an extended image, giving space to the landscape in an asymmetrical composition. This was clearly too radical for the time and his canvases have been cut into sections by others who sought to correct his composition and make the figures more central. He was out of kilter with accepted norms and it was suggested that his work 'satisfies neither a taste for what is loosely but confidently referred to as pictorial unity, or a taste for narration'.[11] What is interesting in this argument is that the asymmetry might have made it easier for Tiepolo to marry his painting to an architectural structure. The fresco seems to tune into the architectural form, playing games at times, but allowing the eye to dart across the surface without a single point of focus, or adhering to accepted rules of composition. He seems to have thrived on the idea of movement and interconnection with architecture and light. He was also known to work quickly and to be

accommodating in his practice, perhaps suggesting that he had an aptitude for working collaboratively with the architect.

At Würzburg, the painting is a mixture of fresco – pigment applied to wet lime plaster – then secco, detail added once the plaster was dry with pigment in an organic binder, such as tempera or oil. In general, pigments applied to dry plaster are less durable. The choices of colour are particularly interesting in terms of the depiction of light and shadow within the painting and from the local light sources coming from the windows in the hallway. The colour palette for the painting is grounded by earth pigments of ochre, umbers, green and red earths, forming a muddy field over which darker and more expensive pigments, such as vermilion, would be added to enliven and energise. The intense moments of colour then grab attention and invite the eye to dart across the vast surface, stopping on one figure then the next. Because the artist had been working in an adjacent space and therefore passed through the stairway daily for two years before starting the commission, he would have been aware of the passage of light across the seasons and the movement of people in the space. The vast flat curve of the vault was lit by high-level windows on three sides, but the orientation of the windows casts a very different light quality onto the ceiling. The windows to the north face a courtyard space where the sandstone walls reflect a warm ochre tone into the space, with the void space acting as 'a form of solar reservoir'.[12] The other windows are not regularly located. It is useful to understand that these differences in the colour temperature of the daylight (warm or cool white) from each direction would be superimposed on the painting and modify the colour appearance. Tiepolo clearly adjusted the composition and the placing of specific figures and their colour to respond to the changing light conditions. The painting affords multiple readings depending on the time of year and the angle of the sun. The deep reveals of the oval windows would moderate some of the intensity of the sunlight. More significantly, some of the windows were boarded up after the death of the architect and artist, and a clumsy cornice added, which obscures some of the painting and contradicts a virtual cornice that had already been part of the fresco.

LEFT

2.4   Staircase at the Residenz, Würzburg by Balthasar Neumann, with vaulted ceiling painting by Giovanni Battista Tiepolo, 1751–3

The painting is carefully situated to take account of the angle of view and the changing perspective as the observer moves up the first stair, turning through 180 degrees to climb the second flight on one side or other. It is impossible to see the painting as a whole and this is evidently anticipated, even though the artists would have been working on a boarded scaffolding in dust and discomfort, without being able to see the effect of the painting as we do now. The narrative in the painting is unveiled as the body moves through the space and different figures appear or take prominence. Alpers' and Baxendall's analysis also confirms that the figures themselves have been adjusted and foreshortened to take account of the upward perspective. This painting was never intended to have a static reading, neither in terms of the way the eye crosses the surface, nor in terms of the dynamic light conditions. Like all great Baroque architecture, it invites the viewer to drift into an infinite space above. It responds to its architectural setting through subtle interplay between the physical form, the human experience and the environmental conditions of light and orientation.

In 2013, the Scottish artist and writer, John Byrne (b. 1940) was invited to make a painting, *All the World's a Stage* (fig.2.5), on the domed ceiling at the King's Theatre in Edinburgh.[13] The commission followed two notable mid-20th-century examples of large-scale domed ceiling paintings in Paris: Marc Chagall's then controversial painting at the Opéra Garnier (1964), and Andre Masson's intervention at the Théâtre de L'Odéon (1965), which negotiated the vast circular surfaces high above the auditoriums. Unlike the staircase at Würzburg, these surfaces are seen by a predominately static audience and the architectural form is contained by the circular shallow dome. The angle of view is highly significant, seen from below and in low light. The composition can therefore be more self-referential, but still has to adjust to work with the scale and three-dimensional form of the surface.

At the time of each commission both Chagall and Byrne were in their 70s, and the scale and physical demands of painting must have been daunting. The method of making the paintings on the surface is very different in each case. Chagall took over nine months to complete the paintings with an assistant, painting on canvas in sections in his studio. The work was then stretched over a frame set below the existing ceiling, thereby retaining the pre-existing painting above. It was such a controversial commission that perhaps this method was conceived to allow it to be removed, but more likely it was for logistical reasons: to allow the artists to work more comfortably and to allow the Opéra to continue in use. Byrne's work, by contrast, was painted directly onto the surface by a team of assistants over a tight five-week period, using contemporary technology to project a gridded image onto the surface. Computer modelling also helped match the circular painting to the three-dimensional surface of the dome. Byrne's work is notable not only for its size, extending to 85 square metres, but also because it is figurative, appropriately theatrical and celebratory. Byrne is also a playwright with a passion for theatre, making this commission a perfect match. In terms of the composition, the work carefully negotiates the curvature of the surface, with the figures emerging through traditional forms of swirling clouds around the circumference. The most detailed sections of the figures are painted on the flatter sections to reduce the distortion, but also to make them least obscured from all areas of the seating below. Byrne joined the team to work on the detail, overpainting in oils over a base in acrylic to achieve a crisp level of detail (fig.2.6). The two main figures – a black harlequin who cradles the sun and a red-haired woman reaching to the moon – denote day and night. Achieving an appropriate scale for the figures was essential, given the height of the surface above the audience. In these theatre settings, there is no daylight and they come to light and life for a performance. In terms of colour, the work is joyful and vibrant. It intensifies the architecture of the already exuberant neo-Baroque styled interior and heightens the shared experience of the theatre.

When making easel art, the artist cannot predict the light conditions in which it will be viewed, or the colour temperature of the light source. In architectural settings, light – particularly daylight – will be variable, but the fluctuations predictable within a range, giving an opportunity to observe the surface react and adjust to the site conditions. For example, two large wall murals by Peter Lanyon from the 1960s sit in a dialogue with their surroundings. Lanyon (1918–64) studied at Euston Road School and was taught by Victor Pasmore

2.5   John Byrne, *All the World's a Stage*, King's Theatre, Edinburgh, 2013

2.6   John Byrne working on his dome ceiling mural, King's Theatre, Edinburgh, 2013

2.7   Peter Lanyon, wall painting at the University of Birmingham Faculty of Arts, 1963,
oil on board, 259.1 × 513.1 cm (102 × 202 in)

and Ben Nicholson. For Lanyon, the 'sense of place' was fundamental to his art, and environmental conditions – wind, weather, waves and the power of nature – were consistent themes evoked in his brush strokes. The situation for each mural would have a profound effect on the development of the artwork, not only because of the light, but because of the function of the space, views in and out, and the need for durability. In 1959, at the University of Liverpool Civil Engineering Building, working with the architects Fry, Drew, Drake and Lasdun, his preference would have been to use paint on a canvas, but the university demanded that the mural should be 'student proof' and it was changed to ceramic tiles. It is set in an artificially lit hall space with little daylight, and is still intact and treasured by the institution. In contrast, the mural for the University of Birmingham Faculty of Arts building, completed in 1963 (fig.2.7), was set on the side wall of the reception space looking directly into a courtyard and flooded with light. The

views to and from the grassy courtyard are sensed in the arrangement of the colour, with the green landscape invited into the composition. Lanyon's technique was to paint the mural off-site in sections, so it is not on the wall surface as such. However, the work was tested through paper sketches and adjusted to suit the site-specific conditions. Both colour and the disposition of the forms went through a radical change between the studies and the final painting. Lanyon's fascination with weather conditions, time and movement are captured on the surface of his canvas. As noted by Mo Enright, it seems clear that the studies were not an 'exact blueprint for the final work'.[14] From an architect's point of view, it seems strange that, despite the care taken to adjust the colour and composition, the artist was not concerned with a clash with the architectural elements, namely a doorway to the right end of the wall. Why does the canvas extend up and over the door? Would it not feel more comfortable to stop in line with the frame? Or if it did, would this suggest it was a planted easel painting rather than fully occupying and integrated with the wall? Both murals have survived, but must now contend with dropped ceilings adjacent to the work, which would not have been there at the time of creation. As students and staff come and go, the wall paintings will be anchored in their collective memories of these spaces.

COMPLEXITIES AND CONTRADICTIONS

Much of the discomfort that architects may feel about wall paintings, and even the application of colour, is that it will distort the reading of the form. Colour has a dynamic quality which, even when applied in pure flat planes and restricted to the boundaries of the wall and ceilings, has a spatial effect. Colour and pattern have the ability to alter the appearance not only of the surface itself, but beyond the surface, to affect the perception of the space. Applied decoration, either in the form of a layer of paint or through an embedded artwork, may invoke tensions between the reading of the form and that of the surface, and by extension between the artist and the architect.

The uneasy relationship between architectural form and surface is far from a modernist or contemporary dilemma. Antonio Foscari relates Andrea Palladio's struggle to wrestle some sense of control over surface decoration through fresco paintings at the Villa Foscari (Malcontenta) (1557–75).[15] The author argues that Palladio, who identified himself as an architect, would have preferred to avoid any adornment to the whitewashed walls and vaulted ceilings of his clients' villas, and in some cases he succeeded. The simplicity of the unadorned structure is evident in the lower ground floor of the villa. While clients may have employed him specifically because he offered a radical new style, a complete lack of ornamentation may have been too disconcerting. Rather than have the central hall disfigured by incompatible figurative images, the author suggests that Palladio, somewhat reluctantly, collaborated with the painter Battista Zellotti (one of a succession of artists employed by the client due to changing

family circumstances) to ensure that the visual integrity of the architectural form was consistent with the imagery of the fresco. It may also have had an element of practical self-interest: to maintain a good relationship with a client who might then commission further work. It is interesting to note that while the figures in the frescoes have strong chromatic hues, the architecture represented in the paintings is depicted in white (fig.2.8). The predominance of the white background supports an impression of lightness. A particular tension arises between perspectival representation and actual form. In the case of the large south-facing rooms, the painted images of architecture are symmetrical, even though the actual architecture is not. Depth is implied with figures, depicted with legs dangling over the virtual architecture of the painting. Foscari suggests that Palladio was very conscious that architecture is reliant on an internal discipline and principles that 'regulate its composition', and that the two media – art and architecture – if not handled with sensitivity, may become 'locked in insoluble antagonism'; he continues, 'indeed, Palladio wanted at all costs to avoid a situation in which the introduction of the medium of painting, and the creation of illusory architectural ornamentation to frame the figurations, might alter or, worse still, contradict the essential meaning of his architecture'.[16]

2.8 Frescoes by Battista Zellotti at Andrea Palladio, Villa Foscari, Italy, 1557–75

When the art is gestural, figurative or narrative, there is more to consider. Eric Alliez and Jean-Claude Bonne provide a careful and critical reading of the large mural painting, *The Dance* by Henri Matisse, completed in 1933 for the Barnes Foundation in Philadelphia.[17] It is located on the upper walls of a large room which has three arched vaults. It seems to sit in an extremely uncomfortable position, despite being carefully composed by the artist through a series of painted studies. The grey figures of the dancers in the painting appear to be trying to leap out of the cramped space, and some are even cut off by the architecture. The flat colour of the ground behind is crossed by pink, blue and black-striped forms. It looks even more incongruous when seen in the full elevation of the wall now that the lower walls are off-white, the windows framed by timber surrounds and a series of conventionally hung framed paintings desperately vie for attention with the joyful movement in the Matisse above. From an architect's point of view, it is hard to understand what Matisse was thinking of with this composition. By forcing the figures to be contorted by the architectural form, are we made more aware of the arches? Do the figures leap to escape each other and the ceiling? The contemporary artist Michael Craig-Martin will often make a composition which deliberately introduces tension between the architecture and the art, in which his figurative everyday objects will cross over an architectural feature such as a door surround or fold around a corner (see fig.7.14). His wall paintings seem to agitate the architecture to the point of domination in some cases. But is that his point? An easel painting does not have this option. It will be moved; it is nomadic and so cannot anticipate a specific dialogue – even an antagonistic one. Matisse's work epitomises 'free' non-representational colour, and we can be in no doubt that the choice and placing is spatial. Matisse considered colour to be liberating, but the dynamic dancing figures are in grey while their background is vibrant pink and blue. It seems a curious composition. While the painting pushes the architectural form of the arches to the fore, this could have been achieved more simply with colour, and the painting might seem less compromised on a flat canvas. Achieving a sense of designed unity between artwork and architectural surface is clearly not an easy task.

When colour wraps across the surface of architectural elements – for example, between wall and ceiling – it can force a spatial re-reading that can create an illusion of volume. Haus Auerbach (1924) in Jena, Germany, designed by architects Walter Gropius and Adolf Meyer in a collaboration with the artist Alfred Arndt, uses colour both to imply volume and also to direct the gaze and give orientation and hierarchy within the spaces (fig.2.9). It is an elegant application that seems perfectly in tune with the composition, even though the visual reading of the space is not aligned with the boundaries of walls and ceiling. At the Bauhaus, led by Gropius at this time, wall painting was a significant part of the curriculum and the courses led by Hinnerk Scheper and Wassily Kandinsky. The significance of the Bauhaus in terms of the integration of colour across the arts is extremely well documented elsewhere and remains highly influential and relevant a century later.[18] Scheper's focus was on the practical application of colour in the design of space. He taught that colour should not dominate as a design element, but rather that its application should be led by the architectural elements.

At the Café Aubette in Strasbourg (1927–8), Theo van Doesburg, Hans Arp and Sophie Taeuber-Arp (fig.2.10) made a series of wall and ceiling paintings that sat so uncomfortably with the expected reading of architectural form that they were later destroyed and reinstated in phases, only completing in 2016. Particularly disturbing to the viewer is the clash of geometries in the main 'Ciné-Dancing' hall by van Doesburg. At first sight, it appears as though the colour and geometry wrap from wall to ceiling surfaces, ignoring the corners of the room. Looking more closely, however, this is largely an illusion generated by the geometry of the diagonals set against the vertical and horizontal lines.

The colour does not actually fold, although that is the initial impression. Van Doesburg's unfolded study painting makes this clear (fig.2.11), but the colour design seems all the more disjointed because the pattern is cut off in line at the wall to ceiling junctions. The dislocation of form and colour is accentuated by a three-dimensional relief. The surface treatment acknowledges the corners of the volume, but neither geometry nor colour

2.9   Walter Gropius and Adolf Meyer with artist Alfred Arndt, Haus Auerbach, Germany, 1924

2.10 Theo van Doesburg, with Hans Arp and Sophie Taeuber-Arp, Café Aubette, Strasbourg, 1927–8

2.11   Theo van Doesburg, design for ceiling and walls of Café Aubette, Strasbourg, 1927–8, Galerie Gmurzynska

panels line through. The floor pattern conflicts again, taking its orientation to match the walls and seating carrels. Ultimately, the painting appears to fight with the architecture as though it is trying to escape the container. Further dislocation in the project was caused by different members of the team undertaking separate rooms in the sequence of spaces, without any apparent collaboration. In other rooms, the geometry is more in tune with the form, with each elevation – including the ceiling – designed as a composition. Although the project is jointly attributed, each space seems to have been approached as a discrete volume, and the applied painting developed in response, thereby accentuating the clashing geometry and stylistic approaches.

But the Café Aubette was never intended to be a restful place; one was expected to feel enveloped and dominated by the art. Theo van Doesburg was

so disheartened by the reception of his largest experiment that he retreated to the comparative safety of easel painting. Discussing the architectural projects of the de Stijl group, notably the Rietveld House in Utrecht (1924), which set them apart from the architects of the period, Mark Pimlott concludes that 'the status of art as support for architecture was inadequate to their ambitions'.[19] Colour was emancipated and could have its own rhythm of planes and a synthesis of architectural form. Art was thought to be a way in which the architecture could be deconstructed, or subverted, or that the use of colour through the artwork would make invisible characteristics visible. Today, the Café Aubette survives as an important example of the de Stijl period, and its dissonant composition is the very reason for its status. The audience has been modified by a historical re-reading which sets the paintings in a social and cultural frame; the tensions between the surfaces are anticipated as an artistic curiosity. Pimlott notes an exemplar of the period as the *Proun* works by the Russian avant-garde artist El Lissitzky, which presented a 'dematerialised architecture without resorting to formlessness'.[20]

The wall and ceiling paintings by Swiss-American artist Fritz Glarner for Nelson A. Rockefeller's New York apartment (1964), have a calmness despite their enveloping form, with small areas of red, blue, yellow and black against grey and white (fig.2.12).[21] The five surfaces of the room were composed as a unified artwork allowing each panel to be seen in relation to each other. The surfaces are inscribed by a textured relief which is non-rectilinear and sets the artwork as subtly distinct from the architectural form. A more recent example of a painting that envelopes surfaces is at the Kix Bar in Vienna, by the artist Oscar Putz (1986). The applied painting

2.12   Fritz Glarner, *Rockefeller dining room*, 1964, detail of reconstructed room at the Museum Haus Konstructiv, Zurich

2.13   Oscar Putz, Kix Bar,
Vienna, 1986

2.14 and 2.15 Felice Varini, *Trois Triangles Bleus*, Osaka, 2007, Exposition: The Osaka Art Kaleidoscope

is disruptive in the sense that it folds and wraps around walls and ceilings, but it respects certain architectural lines, doorways, windowsill lines and wall thicknesses. Instead of clashing, the architecture is intensified by the painting. In places it sets a datum, using a horizontal division between colours to define a volume that contains the seated people. This accentuates the height and loftiness of the volume above their heads. Unlike the Café Aubette, colour wraps up a wall and across a ceiling – but does align (fig.2.13). It feels stable and dynamic at the same time. The psychic effect of the polychromy affects the physical reading of surface and implies volumes within the space where there are none, but only to the extent of making the viewer more attentive to the play of light and shadow, or to the thickness of a wall. The choice of the colour palette is also a factor. There is a chalkiness to the colours, which are saturated, but not clear. This anchors them to the wall and they appear fused to the surface. These last two examples exemplify the potential for a layer of applied surface colour to act together with the architectural form but offer a different spatial experience. It is generally the case that architects are more comfortable with polychromy used in this way, as will be discussed in the following chapter.

The French artist Felice Varini takes the optical experience of surface and form to extremes. As noted earlier, the expectation of the easel artist is that there is a fixed gaze, normally in front of the painting, even if first approached from the side. Varini, by contrast, forces multiple spatial readings of the architectural form through anamorphosis until the sweet spot is reached and the painted elements align into a recognisable whole. These are quirky paintings, often executed in places of movement (figs 2.14 and 2.15). The optical illusion can only be fully experienced within the space in which they have been made. As conceptual pieces they re-construct the space around the moment of conjunction, but are perhaps most interesting in the distributed mode as flecks of colour floating on the surface of beams and columns. They interact with space and surface, but also with movement and time.

Returning then to Fernand Léger's definition of 'mural art' – the aim is to introduce art in a unified composition with the architectural context. Perhaps the best examples of surface-applied art in architecture are those where there is a resolution that has a resonance, but also an element of dissonance that achieves a productive tension. The artist Antoni Malinowski, whose work is interwoven through this book, has made a series of ceiling paintings in theatre buildings, the majority in collaboration with the architects Haworth Tompkins (fig.2.16).[22] What makes his ceiling paintings unusual is that he undertakes them alone and in situ in response to the light conditions and the architectural surface. He seeks a way of enriching the architecture, of intensifying the form and the experience of the space through the colour. His technique, layering pigments of varying light reflectance, was used in an early installation at the Bush Theatre, London in 2011. Almost unnoticed, unless the eye drifts upwards, the ceiling paintings nonetheless have a presence in the foyer space, catching and reflecting the light across the surfaces. A deep blue wall painting, flecked with silver and yellow, is sited in a window to wrap the occupants of a small table – the pigments appear

2.16   Antoni Malinowski, wall painting at the Bush Theatre, London, Haworth Tompkins, renovated and extended 2017

to vibrate as light moves across the surfaces and is absorbed or released back into the space.

As part of the restoration of the Chichester Festival Theatre, 2014, originally designed by the architectural practice Powell & Moya and completed in 1962, Malinowski was commissioned to make a ceiling painting in the foyer spaces (fig.2.17). In this case, although the overall theatre architectural form is strongly geometrical, derived in plan from two interlocking hexagons overlaid with a diamond, the foyer ceiling is not a pure form. The ceiling painting plays with this irregularity by introducing a tapering border of vermilion red. Malinowski bemoans our inadequacy of language for colour, preferring to use musical terms to try to explain his process. In terms of the palette, he

will first consider the tone as the equivalent of the musical key. The palette is then restricted and starts with a chord from which everything else will follow. At Chichester, these are red-brown and ochre tones, darker and lighter with a metallic pale bronze contained by a vibrant red curtilage. Triangular flecks of colour produce rhythms and micro-rhythms in the changing light conditions.

The final example here of the use of contemporary architectural surfaces as sites for artwork is the Everyman Theatre in Liverpool, also designed by architects Haworth Tompkins. It was completed in 2014 and subsequently awarded a raft of architectural awards including the RIBA Stirling Prize. The theatre company is a well-loved institution in the city, and part of the brief for the extensive renovation of the building was to make a series of publicly accessible and welcoming front-of-house spaces directly on the street. The building sits on Hope Street, which runs from the Anglican Cathedral to the south; and to the north, the street frames a significant vista to the Metropolitan Cathedral. At both ends of the street, the eye drifts upwards to take in the height of the spires. The most significant surface here is the street facade of the theatre, approached at an acute angle. The upward gaze is directed by the emblematic facade of the theatre (fig.2.18). The *Portrait Wall* is a

LEFT

2.17   Ceiling painting by Antoni Malinowski, Chichester Festival Theatre, Haworth Tompkins, renovation (2014) of Powell & Moya theatre (1962)

BELOW

2.18   Everyman Theatre, Liverpool, street view at dusk, Haworth Tompkins, 2013

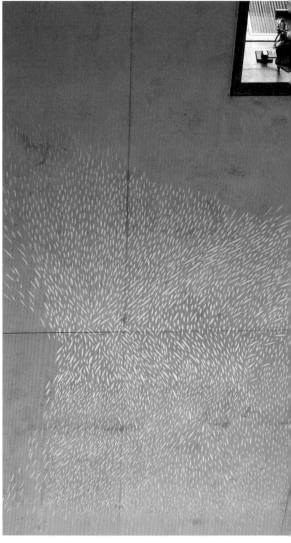

LEFT

2.19 Everyman Theatre, Liverpool, 2013, architects Haworth Tompkins; ceiling paintings by Antoni Malinowski

RIGHT

2.20 Everyman Theatre, Liverpool, 2013, architects Haworth Tompkins; copper ceiling painting by Antoni Malinowski

permanent, collaboratively produced artwork that has become a city landmark. Based on portraits of 105 'everyday' people, the anodised and etched aluminium screen is symbolic of the theatre's inclusive mission. The life-size photographic portraits by Dan Kenyon are abstracted and cut as perforated/slotted silhouettes on rotating shutters stacked in three rows across the full facade. The figures make references to the saints and stone carvings of craftspeople that one finds on the cathedrals, but here the aim was to select a diverse secular portraiture. The silver colour of the facade is subtly varied due to the manufacturing process that gives texture and changes with the daylight, affording protection from excessive sunlight. At night the facade is transformed and illuminated with blue and white light that spills across the street; reflections are particularly vivid when the pavements are wet.

The next most critical surface is the ceiling of the upper foyer bar, with paintings by Malinowski inviting the eye to look up through the figurative screen, attracted by an intense pinkish-red. These are experienced in the periphery of vision or discovered while sitting in the bar. As the daylight diminishes, the pink turns to a deep saturated red in the warm illumination (fig.2.19). The layering of pink, red and purplish brown is unexpected and slightly dissonant. Two techniques are used: tiny flecks of copper that catch the light are brushed directly onto the concrete surface (fig.2.20) and the main paintings are set into the deep recesses between concrete beams.[23] The ceiling has a curious, fluffy texture as the pigment has been soaked into a sound-absorbing material to counteract the hard finishes. Inside the foyers and in the theatre itself, the surfaces are calm, with a material-based palette of exposed concrete, untreated plywood, wood floors, reclaimed brick, black-painted steel and black-glazed bricks. The relatively few painted surfaces are in blocks of chalky green, black and red.

The sonority that Malinowski seeks in his work resonates between the two-dimensional surface and the three-dimensional space, to force perspectival shifts and oscillate the viewer's attention between accentuated surfaces. His influences include Giotto, Tiepolo's fresco painting and Roman wall painting. The painting creates a space and the viewer moves within that space. He is conscious of working within an ancient tradition and that there are few contemporary artists who could endure such hard physical work, painting directly onto the surfaces, adjusting as the artwork develops. A painting is not pre-determined, but evolves in the making: colour and composition are developed and layered in response to the light and the optical sensations that are created. For Malinowski, the fundamental quality of working within architecture is the opportunity to observe the form, the rhythms of structure and the way the light works in the space: 'a painter looks at edges, tiny things, but those tiny things are in some way equally important to the overall geometry'.[24] For the Everyman Theatre ceilings, for example, the colour is set between the concrete beams, it pushes the rhythm of the structure to the fore, making it more apparent. As evident in Tiepolo's Würzburg Residenz ceiling, Malinowski is interested in the way that the architectural surfaces are experienced through peripatetic perception, and incorporates the movement into the composition while he works in the space. He seeks a counterpoint to the architecture to find a moment when the combination begins to resonate. An artwork may draw our attention to the architecture, may adjust the reading of the surface, and the use of colour will alter the experience of the space. The distinctive opportunity afforded by architectural surfaces is therefore ultimately not about the surface per se, but as a setting for artwork that will contribute to the perception of the entire architectural environment.

INNERE ANSICHT DES EMPFANGSSAALES.

3.1 Karl Friedrich Schinkel, *Inner View of the Reception Hall on the Acropolis in Athens*, 1834

3   Architects as Spatial Painters

While much of this book explores collaborations between architects and artists, an architect who has the skill and confidence to use colour may find a collaboration with an artist to be unnecessary, or even a hindrance. This chapter will consider exemplar projects by four architects from the mid-19th century to the present day, all of whom draw on a parallel artistic practice to employ a painterly approach to colour and polychromy.

SCHLOSS CHARLOTTENHOF – A COLLABORATION IN ARCADIA

The 19th-century architect Karl Friedrich Schinkel was an accomplished painter. His skill as a draughtsman and his artistic vision was exemplified in his set designs for the operatic stage. In almost every scene, the viewer gazes out from darkness to light. The view is constructed and framed by an architectural foreground, a deep-set portico or colonnade being a consistent technique. In his artwork, colour is used primarily in support of the tonal contrasts, or to convey a narrative. To what extent might his skill in using colour in his architecture have been learnt through his easel paintings, watercolours and gouaches? Is a painterly approach apparent? The discussion will focus on one of his projects – Schloss Charlottenhof at Potsdam, south of Berlin.

Schloss Charlottenhof was designed for Crown Prince Friedrich Wilhelm on a site to the south-east corner of the Sanssouci estate in Potsdam, which was gifted from his father, King Friedrich Wilhelm III, in 1825. An original manor house on the site was rebuilt and re-configured by Schinkel between 1826 and 1829 by adding a classical portico to the east to address a long, artificially raised garden, and a curved bay window facing north. Approaching from the south, an avenue of four lines of trees leads from dark green shade into light. The house, set to the north, has cream walls and pale blue and white shutters, accentuating the bright contrast of intense sunlight when seen from the canopy of the trees. A high, brown brick wall, topped with a colonnaded pergola, crosses the line of vision, preventing a view into the privacy of the elevated garden. Approached from the north or east, the contained formal garden precedes the house. The portico gives deep shade, framed with blue walls and bound by a frieze of dark grey panels, further deepening the sense of shadow (fig.3.2). Looking up, the soffit is lined with a rectangular grid of recessed, pale blue-green panels and fine brown-red lines. In common with many of Schinkel's drawings and paintings, the views from inside to

3.2 Karl Friedrich Schinkel, Schloss Charlottenhof (1826–9), East Portico

outside frame lightness with darkness. As we look from shade into light, columns become silhouetted, defining an edge to mediate between these worlds. So far, therefore, it is the tonal contrasts, rather than any significance of hue, that defines the composition and the framed view.

Depending on the season, the time of day and weather conditions, the entrance hall to the house completely changes in appearance. Set on the west side, in the morning, even with white upper walls and ceiling, it is dark and unwelcoming. A substantial change in level puts the visitor at a distance, inferior to the host. In the afternoon, an intense blue light floods the space from a fanlight set above the door (fig.3.3). The atmosphere of the space is transformed in the blue light and it feels positively watery. The floor and wall paintings refer to Schinkel's visit to the ruins of Pompeii.[1] Antique marbles in green, black and white, and red-brown Silesian marble, line the floor and continue across the lower walls. The most public room, a large dining room, sits on this axis. A strong vermilion red fabric is used to line the interconnecting double door frames, and when opened, the doors frame a view to the luscious green of the landscape beyond. Each colour, blue to red to green, is highly saturated.

In plan, the sequence of rooms places day rooms and the guest rooms to the south, with the most private rooms across the north end, which would be bypassed by most visitors. The north-facing main bedroom is flanked either side by two gendered studies, male and female. The study for Crown Prince Friedrich Wilhelm has mid-tone saturated green walls, lined with gold detail at wall to cornice junctions and vertically at the corners. This gilt lining is repeated throughout the building. A hidden stair, leading from the adjacent bedchamber down to the floor below, is disguised as a cabinet. The green – originally Schweinfurt/Paris green, which was a highly toxic copper and arsenic compound – continues into the north-facing main bedchamber, with a semi-circular bow window connecting to the green of the landscape beyond. The green is further reflected in the mirror panels set into the doors, wrapping the occupants in a verdant cocoon. The Crown Prince adopted the name 'S.I.A.M.' for Schloss Charlottenhof. The four letters referred to the Kingdom of Siam (now Thailand) and to the concept of an Arcadian model of an idyllic life,

free from politics. For the couple, the modestly scaled house served as a retreat from royal duties into nature. The ceilings and cornices are generally white, with a warm red-brown colour coming from the parquet timber floor which runs throughout the house. Much of the furniture was designed by Schinkel and made in mahogany and maple. The doors vary throughout the house; some are walnut, some white, glazed, mirrored, silver and gilt, or lined in fabric. An anteroom off the entrance hall was used as a reception space and, with fawn-coloured walls, appears bland in contrast to the rest of the apartments. From here, one door leads into the living room, the other to the Crown Prince's study.

When interconnecting doors are opened, the appearance immediately shifts from monochromatic rooms to a polychromatic promenade. One colour frames the next. The interaction of the colours also becomes apparent and heightens the experience. For example, from the green/gold bedchamber, the adjacent pink/silver room is seen (figs 3.4 and 3.5). This was designed as a study for Crown Princess Elizabeth. A deeper blue-green is introduced on the door facings and lined with silver. Beyond that, a pale blue is used in the east-facing living room, leading through to the large dining room, where the vermilion doors, lined with felt and studded with gold, frame distance views through to two further rooms – known as 'cabinets'. In the corners of the dining room, semi-circular niches are also lined in vermilion, domed with dark blue and gold stars – most famously used by Schinkel in the set for the Palace of the Queen of the Night in Mozart's opera, *The Magic Flute*. When the connecting door to the entrance hall is opened, there is a view to the fanlight that repeats the deep blue and gold stars. The rooms are hung with numerous etchings of Switzerland and northern Italy, reminding the couple of past travels. The first of the cabinet rooms, set to the south of the dining room, is a soft, chalky green colour, seen through the red-lined double doors; then finally on this long north–south axis, there is a magenta-red room which was used as a breakfast room, with an east-facing window providing a deep view along a colonnaded pergola. The space immediately outside this room is thrown into deep shadow by both an oversailing roof and flanking walls, with very dark brown-black stained

RIGHT

3.3　Karl Friedrich Schinkel, Schloss Charlottenhof, view from dining room into west entrance hall, flooded with blue tinted light

LEFT

3.4   Karl Friedrich Schinkel, Schloss Charlottenhof, detail of decoration

RIGHT

3.5   Karl Friedrich Schinkel, Schloss Charlottenhof, polychromatic promenade

3.6   Karl Friedrich Schinkel, Schloss Charlottenhof, south cabinet room with dark pearwood doors

pearwood doors edged in gilt to accentuate the contrast (fig.3.6). This would serve to increase the effect of darkness to light and the lush water garden beyond. Originally, the red was intended to be carmine, a red lake pigment imported from South America, but was changed to a wallpaper.[2] The interaction of colour here is clearly intended to include the external views, bringing the natural colours of the landscape into the composition.

Most curiously, the promenade sequence then leads to a guest bedroom decked with blue and white canvas draped in the form of a tent. This seems whimsical and not in keeping with the rest of the house. It is, however, highly theatrical and was fashionable in the 18th to 19th centuries. The styling was thought to have originated in a design for Napoleon in the Malmaison Palace near Paris.[3] Finally, the 'Ladies sitting room' is accessed directly from the entrance hall and from the Tent room, and has off-white walls with a large, glazed, tiled stove. As with the reception room on the north side of the hall, this guest space lacks character in comparison to the private quarters.

The nearby bathhouse complex is directly inspired by Schinkel's visit – around 1804 – to the Roman remains at both Herculaneum and Pompeii. The vermilion, black and green painted entrance room bridges the formal rose garden to the south and the deep-set, dark baths to the north. The baths are open to the air through voids in the roof. Although the main walls are painted with motifs, Klaus Jan Philipp suggests that Schinkel was less interested in the decorative art of the Roman villas,

LEFT

3.7   Karl Friedrich Schinkel, red wall painting in the Roman style, Bath House, Sanssouci, Potsdam

ABOVE

3.8   Karl Friedrich Schinkel, caryatids with roof opening, Bath House, Sanssouci, Potsdam

but more enamoured by the colouring of the walls and the floor mosaics.[4] The red here is a bright red-orange hue, more akin to a Cinnabar red, which is known to have been used in Roman villas along with manufactured Egyptian blue, carbon black and ochres (figs 3.7 and 3.8). The apparent depth and darkness of the interior rooms is strengthened by a deep aqua green-blue and umber on the walls, with fine white lines in the corners and junctions giving the eye some orientation in the penumbra.

Schinkel's use of polychromy in the Schloss Charlottenhof seems to have served a number of purposes. First, and perhaps most commonly, it is used to ascribe character and identity to each space, differentiating between uses. It is used to make links between inside and outside, from a largely monochromatic room to connections out into the landscape. From the green bedroom to the north this is explicit, the room reaching out even further in the curved bay form. In 'Charlottenhof: The Prince, the Gardener, the Architect and the Writer', Iain Boyd Whyte explores the interrelationships between four protagonists in developing this arcadian narrative.[5] The gardener here is Peter Joseph Lenné, who worked on a number of projects with Schinkel, but had already been commissioned to work on the extensive gardens at Sanssouci park for the King. The Roman writer is Pliny the Younger, whose letters had been published as a collection in 1751 and were avidly read by the Crown Prince, who was himself a skilled draughtsman and made around 60 drawings based on the texts. The elevated water garden, for example, seems to have emerged from these studies. Water is repeatedly used as an ordering device and theme throughout the park, in both formal lines and in deliberately informal ponds. Furthermore, from the bedchamber, the theme of life and death is played out by a visual axis between a piped water spring bubbling in the foreground and a gravestone placed on the hilltop in the far distance. It would seem, therefore, that there is more to the choice of green for this room than simply character. It supports a narrative of the cyclical rebirth of nature and invites the outside into the interior.

Next is the use of daylight. From the largely white-painted dining room looking east, the internal hue was perhaps less significant in the composition. The view to the outside is the primary focus and is held back in the deep shadow of the portico and columns; here the contrast is between light and dark. Barry Bergdoll notes that the symbolism of night and day in the house was enhanced over the succeeding decade, including the addition of two medallions by the Danish sculptor Thorvaldsen in the entrance hall.[6] The deep blue exterior walls become deeper in shadow. In one of Schinkel's best-known drawings, the upper gallery of the Altes Museum in Berlin was shown as an intermediate semi-external space in darkness, looking to the Hofgarten and Palace beyond. Schinkel's ink drawings and paintings repeatedly use a very dark tone in the foreground, heightening the experience and depiction of the light beyond. In the case of Charlottenhof, the play of daylight is also tinted with hue. In the late afternoon, the doors to the entrance hall open into an intense blue light, with the polished surfaces reflecting the light further inwards, experienced against the red of the doors.

Finally, colour is used in a theatrical manner to stage a series of constructed vistas in an axial, filmic sequence where the colours interact with each other within the depth of field. As Boyd Whyte

notes, 'starting with the plan, we find Schinkel and Lenné posing an intricate set of questions about the relationship between the path of the body and the path of the eye. The whole complex is designed to be seen on the move.'[7]

The promenades of the park continue internally into the house, but here the use of colour suggests that Schinkel may have been influenced by the work of Johann Wolfgang von Goethe, whose *Farbenlehre* (*Theory of Colours*) had been published in 1810.[8] Schinkel had met Goethe in Weimar in 1816 and again in 1824, so clearly there was scope for an interchange of ideas. Goethe's writings speak to atmospheric conditions and to our experience of colour. In the Schloss Charlottenhof, Schinkel was presented with a unique opportunity to work collaboratively with a group of seemingly like-minded and creative individuals to explore a constructed narrative. Although there is less written on the use of colour within this articulated landscape, the fact that the colour has a strong presence in this composition can be seen as an essential factor in reinforcing the connections between figure and ground, the framed promenade and a heightened experience of changing light conditions.

PAINTERLY PROMENADE AT THE THORVALDSEN MUSEUM, COPENHAGEN

A thread can be drawn between Schinkel, Goethe and the Danish architect Michael Gottlieb Bindesbøll, whose museum for the sculptor Bertel Thorvaldsen in the centre of Copenhagen was completed in 1844 (fig.3.9). The museum integrates colour both externally and internally, and most memorably in a continuous circulation axis, cutting through room to room and forming a circuit around the museum. The young architect is known to have sought out Goethe in Weimar in 1822, while also visiting Schinkel's new buildings in Berlin.[9] He spent time in Rome with Thorvaldsen, who lived and worked there for over 40 years, and while there, in 1824, Bindesbøll met Schinkel.[10] The Grand Tour, and most significantly the first-hand experience of the highly saturated pigments used in

3.9   Michael Gottlieb Bindesbøll, Thorvaldsen Museum, Copenhagen (1844)

polychromatic Grecian colours have recently been restored), but he will have known all about the New Polychromy which sprang from Percier, through Hittorf, Gau and Semper, which was to sweep across the western world during the second quarter of the 19th century, and was to be so triumphantly adopted by Bindesbøll and his team at Thorvaldsen's Museum.[12]

The polychromatic promenade at the museum used only traditional powdered pigments, and with the intention that they would be applied using a wet fresco technique, also learnt from his trip to Italy. The combination of unadulterated pigment and wet plaster would have made the colour more vibrant and the texture more subtle than appears today – replicated in paint. In her book, *Thorvaldsen's Museum: Architecture – Colours – Light*, the architect and colour researcher Bente Lange provides a detailed account of the plaster layers and the original pigments recorded in Bindesbøll's sketches from Pompeii. These were ochre, raw and burnt umber, caput mortuum (a very deep purplish brown achieved by heating ochre to oxidise the iron), earth green, carbon black and ultramarine (figs 3.10–3.12).[13] The wall colours were carried through to the mosaic flooring, much of which has been modified over time.

Thorvaldsen lived just long enough to see the main sections of the museum completed before he died in 1844, although not the final frieze painting by Jørgen Valentin Sonne. On the outside, a strong yellow ochre isolates the museum from the dull grey of the building behind and makes it highly prominent in its surroundings. The colours used in Sonne's frieze were deliberately reduced to yellow, red, green, black and white to accord with the exterior of the building, using a graphic technique similar to the flattened perspective seen on Greek vases. Bindesbøll was aware that the sculptor liked the idea of his work being seen against dark walls, as had been the case when it was shown in an exhibition at Gottfried Semper's pavilion in Altona in 1834. Inside Thorvaldsen's museum, the vaulted ceilings are either a deep ultramarine seen against the caput mortuum, or are decoratively painted with figurative designs, as in an Imperial villa.

Bindesbøll developed the axial plan layout for his competition-winning proposal, cleverly

the Roman villas, alongside Goethe's book *Theory of Colours*, were to affect Bindesbøll at a profound level. He sketched and recorded his travels avidly in notebooks. Indeed, an earlier traveller had been Sir John Soane who, Patrick Baty notes, had managed to acquire a fragment of Herculaneum red plaster, taking it back to London to replicate at his house in Lincoln's Inn Fields, now the Soane Museum.[11] The curator of the Soane Museum, Peter Thornton, writing in 1989, makes this direct connection:

> He [Soane] was a very modern architect in his day. He had not only adopted the rich colour-scale of 'Pompeian' or 'Greek Revival' (for instance, in his Library where the walls are deep red, or at his villa at Ealing where his

FROM LEFT TO RIGHT

3.10   Michael Gottlieb Bindesbøll, Thorvaldsen Museum, Copenhagen, 1844, interior axis

3.11   Michael Gottlieb Bindesbøll, Thorvaldsen Museum, Copenhagen, 1844, corridor to central court

3.12   Michael Gottlieb Bindesbøll, Thorvaldsen Museum, Copenhagen, 1844, main hall space with ultramarine in the window ingoes and caput mortuum on the walls

3.13 and 3.14   Michael Gottlieb Bindesbøll, Thorvaldsen Museum, Copenhagen (1844)

making use of pre-existing masonry walls from the original carriage depot building on the site. This repetitive cellular layout lent itself to the display of the sculptures (figs 3.13 and 3.14). Although the movement from space to space was quite conventional as an enfilade, the visual connection of room to room along the main axes is radically modified by the glimpsed colour, which is then further modified by the constantly shifting direction of sunlight and atmospheric conditions, and suggests that Bindesbøll was making a deliberate interplay between the colour of the individual rooms that was not static. The combination of colours is also significant in this painted promenade, and the room colours are not symmetrically composed despite the axial plan. Bindesbøll overpainted his own line drawings to make lively studies of the transformational effect

of the colour.[14] On one long axis, raw and burnt umber are interspersed with dark ochre and light caput mortuum in tonal shifts, while on the other side, which has more intense daylight, green earth pigment is added to the palette. The interaction between the soft brown reds, greens and yellows is carefully manipulated. Clearly, Bindesbøll's painterly technique was concerned with the materiality of colour and of its application, as well as the composition of a serial experience.

While Schinkel uses colour to link inside to outside, pre-empting a modernist uninterrupted flow of space, Bindesbøll also connects the inner world of the museum to the central court, but using dark tones in window ingoes to make a heavier, thicker boundary between the two. By contrast in the main double-height gallery that faces outwards and south, an intense blue surrounds the high-level windows, suggesting that there is an attempt to dissolve the thickness of the wall into the sky beyond. Both architects were evidently aware of the plastic nature of colour and light. Schinkel makes the movement of sunlight explicit as the blue light suddenly appears in the afternoon in the entrance hall at Charlottenhof. Bindesbøll placed the central windows at a height that would at times highlight the heads of the sculptures around the perimeter on the upper floor, appearing to make them float against the very dark walls.

It is evident from these early 19th-century examples that the architects were using colour to achieve spatial effects using polychromatic interaction. The effect is heightened in both cases by the movement of the viewer through a choreographed sequence of spaces. Distant views foreshorten the colour compositions, while each monochromatic room is experienced along the promenade. The path of the eye is carefully staged, forcing oscillation between near and distance views, while colour reinforces thresholds as part of an aesthetic experience of space.

LE CORBUSIER – A PREFERENCE FOR POLYCHROMY

In common with Schinkel, the Swiss architect, Charles-Édouard Jeanneret, known as Le Corbusier, practised easel painting in parallel with architecture, although he had mixed feelings on artists working directly within architectural settings. Early in his career in 1923 (fig.3.15), he had made his views on figurative murals in architecture very clear: 'let us not scream with frescoes in our apartments and public places, where dignity should reign, since we have finally come to appreciate the mute eloquence of pure proportions'.[15] He did make exceptions, however, showing greater respect for

3.15   Le Corbusier, architectural polychromy at the Villa La Roche, Paris, 1923

his friend, the artist Fernand Léger. Le Corbusier's views on both colour and art in architecture evolved over his lifetime in practice and through successive creative cycles, to the extent that his polemical statements are sometimes paradoxical. In 1948, for example, he added his own mural painting to an earlier building at La Fondation Suisse in Paris from 1933 (fig.3.16).[16]

His easel painting served a different, more exploratory function, as a research tool for his architecture. However, Jean-Louis Cohen and Staffan Ahrenberg highlight that, in this 'secret labour' of painting, distinctive architectural principles were applied. Numerous sketches were made in advance, the order of the execution – lines, forms, volumes, composition and, finally, colour – evinces that 'this serial working stems from an architect's logic and results from a will to master the pictorial project in its entirety, checking and controlling each phase . . . to faithfully transcribe the creative impulse'.[17] By contrast, his artistic mentor, the painter Amédée Ozenfant, would go straight to paint. His relationship with Ozenfant was a generative period in the development of his thoughts on colour, although the partnership dissolved in 1925. His personal treatise continued to develop and was articulated later through the essay *Polychromie Architecturale* (a text written in the early 1930s but not published until after his death in 1965). The essay is included in the 1998 publication by Arthur Rüegg of the well-known 'colour keyboards' for the Salubra wallpaper company.[18] The origins and development of Le Corbusier's tectonic polychromy are thoroughly explored in Jan de Heer's book, *The Architectonic Colour: Polychromy in the Purist Architecture of Le Corbusier* (2009). Our concern here is the painterly use of colour, specifically, where the architect draws on an artistic sensibility and uses it as an integral tool in their skillset.

First, it is notable that Ozenfant and Jeanneret had made a series of easel paintings in the 1920s exploring a repeated composition of form but using radically varied colour palettes. Some studies removed hue almost entirely to focus solely on tone, giving light and shade primacy in the composition. In a review published in *L'Esprit Nouveau* on the occasion of an exhibition of their Purist paintings at the Galerie Druet in Paris,

3.16   Le Corbusier, mural, 1948, in the foyer at La Fondation Suisse, Cité internationale universitaire de Paris, 1933

3.17   Le Corbusier, *Still Life of the Pavilion of L'Esprit Nouveau*, 1924, oil on canvas, 81 × 100 cm (31 ⅞ × 39 ⅜ in)

Maurice Raynal noted that in their paintings 'colour is a strictly material incidental circumstance, with its own identity. Or to put it more concisely, it is a secondary determinant. It cannot be a goal, only a means.'[19] This use of tonal contrast, of light and shade, echoes Schinkel's paintings, even though in Le Corbusier's case, the subject matter is generally figurative. Schinkel would frame a light vista from a dark foreground, giving a sense of depth and awe. The paintings of Caspar David Friedrich, which would place a silhouetted figure seen from behind against a sublime and expansive view of nature, had clearly left an impression on Schinkel.

In Le Corbusier's paintings, and in common with the revolutionary cubist artists of the early 20th century, form takes precedent over any narrative. His use of light and dark tones in the paintings is always in support of the reading of form and volume as a version of chiaroscuro (fig.3.17). It is possible that Le Corbusier may have read Goethe's *Farbenlehre*. The emphasis of the polarities of light and darkness, but also the visual perception of hues, may have been derived from Goethe but only to a limited extent. De Heer observes that although the hue contrasts and characteristics of blue and yellow that were fundamental to Goethe appear to have been adopted by Le Corbusier, he seemed to wilfully supplant red for yellow, while still listing the experiential characteristics Goethe had ascribed to yellow.

This approach seems consistent with the development of his 'polychromie architecturale', at least in his earlier architectural works. It is the ability of a hue to be tonally light or dark that was the main driver, rather than the hue itself. Therefore, we understand his recommendation to employ blue in the shadow and red in the light, furthering the visual contrast. He repeats a common mantra that blue will yield or retreat, while red is fixed. The spatial effects of colour, however, are frequently confused. In particular, there is less understanding of the significance of saturation, in parallel to the tonal value of the hue itself. For

example, a highly saturated or a light-toned blue may appear to advance, while a tonally dark and/or unsaturated red may appear to retreat when seen in an adjacent situation.[20]

For the Maison Guiette (1925–7) in Antwerp (fig.3.18), the colour design appears to have been agreed in collaboration with his client, the artist René Guiette. Contemporaneous sketches that document the proposed scheme are credited to the artist, not to Le Corbusier.[21] Whether the sketches were executed as a record of the conversation or as design preferences led by the artist is not clear. However, the colours used have similarities with Le Corbusier's paintings from the same period, namely, a chalky pink, pale blue, terracotta, umber, black and white.[22] The choice of a very dark umber colour in the living space, seen in a black and

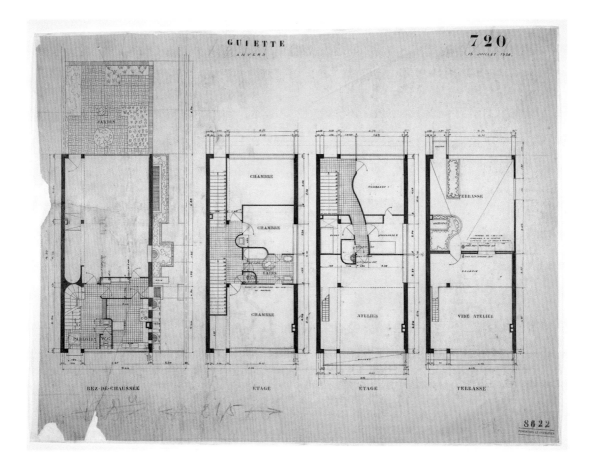

3.18   Le Corbusier with René Guiette, plans of Maison Guiette, Antwerp, 1926

3.19   Le Corbusier with René Guiette, Maison Guiette, Antwerp, 1926, living room,
showing use of dark tone to emphasise form

white photograph (fig.3.19), clearly demonstrates the intention to emphasise the form of a column grid that structures the house in both plan and in section. The record sketch indicates that a grey was first considered for the back wall and columns, but was then changed for the tonally darker umber. The side wall was a pale rose pink and the inside face of the window wall at both ends of the house was a strong blue, that would be seen in deep shadow, in contrast to the daylight beyond. In the stair, blue and reddish hues are combined with white, black and grey (fig.3.20). Although the colour may have been intended to act spatially according to his principles of blue retreating and using sienna red to 'hold' a side wall, here the effect of the tone and saturation suggest a different end result. The pale blue, even in shadow, appears to advance,

while the sienna red is tonally much darker and retreats, especially as it is applied to the soffit of the ceiling as well as the wall. These dynamic, elastic properties of colour were central to the work of the De Stijl group and also to the teaching of colour at the Bauhaus in the same period, led by a series of artists, most notably, Wassily Kandinsky, Oskar Schlemmer, Josef Albers and Johannes Itten. In Kandinsky's case, form and colour were directly related, although it is now thought that he was synaesthetic and therefore may have experienced colour in a more acute, almost transcendental, state.[23] While Josef Albers' *Interaction of Colour* (1963), published much later in his life, remains a seminal text on the effect of adjacent colours in two dimensions, the spatial effects of colour in architectural settings are even more complex.

3.20 Le Corbusier
with René Guiette,
Maison Guiette,
Antwerp, 1926, first-
floor colour design

Context, light conditions, the extent of the colour, the surface reflectance and texture of each material and the properties of the colour itself (hue, tone and saturation) are all interdependent, causing multiple readings of form experienced while moving.

Now turning to the choice of colours, the clearest evidence of Le Corbusier's evolving palette comes from the ranges he curated for the Salubra wallpaper company in 1931 and 1959. Curiously, although the paper was manufactured by an industrial process, a large proportion of the colours in the first range were named to mimic naturally occurring historical and earth pigments, such as burnt sienna, cerulean blue, carmine and red ochre. It would seem that, in this first edition at least, by drawing on the pigments of antiquity as the basis of the palette, contemporary architecture would appear 'eternal' and retain a primary place within the arts.[24] In the first Salubra range, there was no black – only a dark grey – and white was included only as a very pale, creamy yellow. The majority of walls and ceilings at the time would have been covered with white paint, and so a white wallpaper was considered superfluous. There were a few striking exceptions to the earthy palette, such as a strong orange. Curiously, there is no yellow ochre, which was, and remains, one of the most common 'architectural' colours because it is easily sourced. The closest in the Salubra range was a pale, sandy shade. On the selection of the colours, Arthur Rüegg notes that 'they did not take place logically on the basis of an "objective" analysis of harmonic color references, the way it had been [done] before by the German Wilhelm Ostwald, for example'.[25] More significant was the concept that the colours were designed to be 'constructive' in terms of their volumetric appearance – some static, some dynamic. Hence the foundation in the earthy pigments related to their apparent visual stability in comparison to citron yellow, orange and light cobalt blue, which would be more prone to disturb a composition. In the 1959 edition, there are only 20 colours and they are less traditional, suggesting that either Le Corbusier had embraced the contemporary pigment technology, or that the range had been adapted to offer the user a more vibrant experience aligned to changes in market taste between 1931 and 1959. Ivory white and black

were now provided, along with two versions of grey-brown (umbra), and a strong yellow and pink that appeared along with a lively olive green.

In their meticulous analysis of the 1931 Salubra wallpaper range against the Swedish Natural Colour System (NCS) coding, the colour research group led by Juan Serra, provide evidence of Le Corbusier's idiosyncrasies, and the vagaries of his selection.[26] In addition to providing users with sets of colours arranged in themes, Le Corbusier offered a means to combine colours using limited combinations that were deemed to be successful. Unlike paint, where the tone could be easily adjusted on site, the wallpaper had to be manufactured as a standard product, and so a range of tonal values, based on 14 base hues, was provided. The research study confirms the absence of yellow-red and yellow-green hues in the 1931 palette, but also establishes preferences in the suggested colour combinations. For example, Le Corbusier repeatedly suggests combining colours of similar chromaticness (saturation), or from similar hue families, and combinations of warm and cool hue contrasts – but not specifically relating to opponent hues, as was a feature of the writings of both Goethe and the chemist Michel Eugène Chevreul.[27] A key observation linking Le Corbusier's architectural work to his paintings is the regularity of contrasts in the level of NCS 'blackness' value – supporting the significance of light/dark chiaroscuro.

From his own artistic practice Le Corbusier concluded that colour was essentially material, that the appearance of light and shade could be achieved – or given emphasis – through the application of paint. Colour was seen as directly associated with the point of execution, rather than necessary to the idea. Similarly, there is strong evidence that the disposition and juxtaposition of colour as part of a promenade was left until very late in the design process, then decided and executed on site. Only at that point would the lighting and other environmental conditions become realised. This is a common approach for architects, but perhaps misses the opportunity for colour to be used in a conceptual, strategic manner and integral to the design. The emergence of 'plan libre', although understood as a radically different organisation of space, did not seem to make a significant shift in Le Corbusier's choice or use of colour. As part of the sensory experience of his architecture, the eye would be invited to scan and focus on a surface, before sensing a distant point glimpsed or framed as part of the composition. In some projects, Le Corbusier was known to have adjusted the composition on site to emphasise a spatial reading as part of a moving promenade. In a direct reference to his variant paintings that first tested tone, the whole colour design at the Villa Baizeau (1928–30) was adjusted from a predominately white theme to polychrome.[28] Tonal values were tweaked on site to work perpetually with light and dark in support of a particular volumetric or tectonic reading. Dark colours were used to 'correct' an awkward form where it emerged less successfully in the realised project than in design drawings. The darkness would diminish or alter the appearance of the form, and thus minimise clumsy junctions or clarify a particular reading.[29]

In the projects where Le Corbusier was less frequently on site, or had delegated to an assistant such as Alfred Roth, sketches were simply annotated in advance with the proposed colours, even making direct reference to the Salubra codes. This suggests that he made use of the coding as a convenient means of communicating the intention of a colour design when used in an elemental manner, wall by wall, but was less concerned with the observed effect. In his later projects in the 1930s, and particularly post-war, Le Corbusier appears to dispense with the spatial effect of colour altogether. In projects such as the student rooms at the Swiss Pavilion (1933; renovated by the architect in 1957 with a new colour design variant), or the Unité housing at Marseille (1951) and Berlin (1957), there appears to be a more randomised approach. The colours themselves are altogether less subtle, as was the case in the 1959 Salubra range, and he resorted to a colour design that seems driven by hue, and used to differentiate. Although one of the stated aims of the restricted Salubra palette was to allow the user to 'act with security', there is evidence that he made use of the defined colours in his own work, but not in a systematic way, as was urged by the instructions to users.[30] It is possible that the typology of multiple small rooms demanded a different approach. The original Salubra colours had been classified into groups,

some suggesting a mood, while the *Polychromie Architecturale* argues that all colours fall into two main categories – warm and cold – with a broad sensorial association. It could be that he prioritised such subjective associations or had become more interested in the play of light on colour reflected from rough and shiny surfaces, such as along the central corridor in Marseille and in the chapel at the Monastery of La Tourette, completed in 1961. Whatever the reason, although he continued to use colour, it is evident that Le Corbusier did not stick rigidly to any system, preferring to adhere to his mantra that 'to fix rules would be perilous'.[31]

BOLLES+WILSON ARCHITECTS – FROM SHOE POLISH TO RADICAL POLYCHROMY

In common with Schinkel, Bindesbøll and Le Corbusier, the contemporary architects Bolles+Wilson, based in Germany, employ a painterly approach to colour. Peter Wilson has painted since childhood, remarking that it was a form of escape from paternal demands to do sporting activities.[32] Drawing and painting remain central to Wilson's design practice. Recently, hand drawings overlaid with watercolour have become a fast and direct means of communication for the practice's work in Albania, when fees were too low to allow for a full set of conventional architectural drawings and site visits were infrequent. This chapter will argue that this painterly approach allows the semiotic meaning of the image to surface more readily than with architectural line drawings through a self-reflective and interpretive process. The paintings also have the advantage of being inherently coloured from the earliest conceptual stage to completion, meaning that decisions on colour evolve with the design, rather than being applied at a late stage, as is often the case in contemporary practice.[33]

The origins and significance of this artistic, painterly approach are evident in early work by the practice which is seeded with a highly self-aware wit. The publications *Some Reasons for Travelling to Italy* (2016) and *Some Reasons for Travelling to*

Albania (2019) are narrative accounts that tread
a path through historical and political moments,
fleetingly discussed but cumulatively providing
evidence of a deep engagement with the social and
cultural context for the practice's work. The books
offer glimpses into the vast collection of hand
drawings and watercolour paintings that are valued
in their own right alongside the built outputs.

Peter Wilson is renowned for his artistic and
draughting skills, and his drawings have been highly
influential. Early drawings made when he was
studying at the Architectural Association in London
were dense pencil studies of light and shade with
little colour. Finely drawn ink projections would
then be combined with areas of colour block, the
graphic colour throwing the fine drawing to the
foreground. The most dominant use of colour in
these drawings is unrelated to the subject itself;
in some cases the visual order is reversed, with
translucent colour block oversailing the drawing.
Prior to any use of computer drawing and printing,
covering large areas of a drawing on paper
demanded inventiveness with the media. The strong
terracotta colour, which was repeatedly used, was
made with a tan-coloured shoe polish that gave the
right density of dye to the page (fig.3.21). Many of
the drawings from this period are black and white
with restrained areas of lemon yellow, a touch of
turquoise or a splash of vermilion red. Although
the objects and the colour do not always coincide,
the use of colour is part of a narrative. Wilson
continues to tell stories, to spin and to weave an
intellectual investigation through his paintings
and sketchbooks. Much of this, he has noted, are
conversations first with himself, as 'private reveries',
as 'objects or by-products accidentally brought
into being by the hand of the architect'.[34] Unlike
architecture that will take many years to come to
fruition, these are not only representational but
are also intellectual wanderings, and humour and
self-awareness are present in the titles. The series
Small World Theory (2018–19), for example, includes
Freaky Suit Malevich, *Beuys im Knast* (*Beuys in Jail*)
and *Continental Drift and What to Do About It*.

Although the majority of the miniature drawings
and watercolours are not project-related, some
do also communicate directly with their varied
audiences – with his partner Julia Bolles, with office
collaborators, with clients, and more recently in

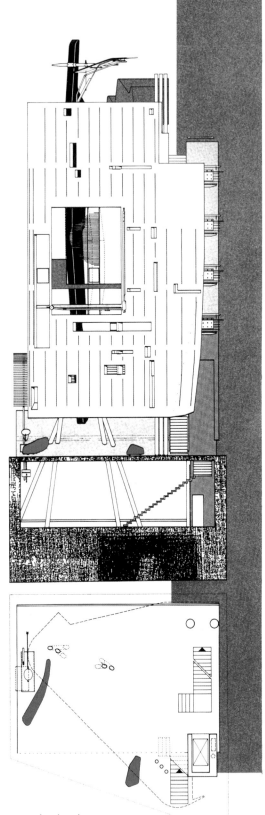

3.21 Bolles+Wilson Architects, *Cosmos Street Office Building Tokyo*, composite elevation
and ground-floor study, ink drawing with tan shoe polish colouring (drawing, c.1989)

the Albanian projects, through hand drawings with craftspeople on site. Unlike Schinkel's lithographs and Le Corbusier's oil paintings on canvas, Wilson's miniature paintings are predominately in watercolour. There is a sense that many are made while travelling, while he himself pauses on a bench, in an exhibition, or at his office desk. The deliberateness of making a painting is significant. In *The Craftsman*, Richard Sennett acknowledges a question posed to him by the philosopher Richard Foley: 'at a point when I was stuck in my work, he asked me, "What is your guiding intuition?" I replied on the spur of the moment, "Making is thinking"'.[35] Painting allows for contemplation and demands a level of commitment, unlike a computer drawing that can be altered instantly. Once a line is drawn, there is no going back. Paint can be superimposed, and perhaps that is where the watercolour may be more forgiving, retaining a level of transparency that allows the line drawing to be overlaid with a less precise medium. Ironically, Wilson was frustrated, but also bemused, by Italian planners for a project in Perugia, Italy who demanded computer drawings for a proposal, implying that they were essentially more accurate than a hand drawing. Anyone who has used computer-aided design (CAD) will know that you get out what you put in, and that may be decidedly inaccurate.

What emerges from this parallel artistic work that transfers into the architectural practice? It is apparent that painting demands colour choice as the very medium and material of expression. The iteration of thousands of small painted studies appears to have given Wilson a confidence and facility as a colourist that is also evident in the architecture of the practice. He feels strongly that architects should be able to work with colour as 'part of their skill set'. He is less comfortable collaborating with artists and sees little need to do so, but he is also very aware that he and Julia Bolles are among the few contemporary architects who continue to make hand drawings, let alone take the time to paint. Other architects including Sheila O'Donnell (O'Donnell and Tuomey) and Steven Holl also continue to use watercolour studies during the design process, and even subsequent to completion, and their architecture usually has a noticeably clear colour strategy. In the commentary that accompanied an exhibition of over 80 of Peter

Wilson's drawings and paintings curated in a solo show in London in 2020, he noted: 'we did not know at the time that a digital eclipse was around the corner. Now some years later some of us pencil-holding dinosaurs are being visited by scholars of ancient technologies.'[36] In the act of painting, one learns how colours mix, how to adjust a hue, tone or saturation, the relative proportions of colour in a composition, how colour will guide the eye across and around the surface, and perhaps most significantly for an architect, how to use colour spatially.

Wilson's sketches and paintings are predominately figurative or exploratory. Colour is used to record what is observed and to differentiate or clarify what is conceived (fig.3.22). This constant activity has been assimilated as an inherent element of the design, so that the architecture without the colour would be unthinkable. It is integral to a way of thinking about both spatial relationships and surface. He observes:

> Colour, considered as applied, suggests a masking, perhaps even deceit. It is also a medium of sensuality, as is form or a

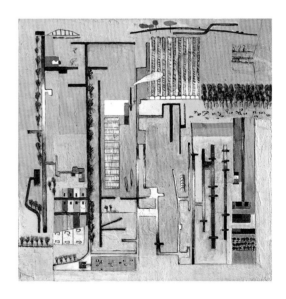

3.22   Peter Wilson, *Missing Sky: Dutch Landscape*, 2001, acrylic and watercolour on primed MDF, 12 × 12 cm (4 ¾ × 4 ¾ in)

tectonically well resolved detail. Over the years I have been training my eye to dwell on nuances of transition, when a tone slips into penumbra or where a wall has faded or been stained. Computer gradations make a mockery of this subtle art.[37]

A concentrated example of this painterly approach is to be found in the city of Korça in post-communist Albania. Korça is the site for a series of architectural projects by the practice. Having previously developed a rapport with the mayor of Tirana, Edi Rama (who subsequently became Prime Minister), the practice won a competition for the masterplan for Korça for mayor Niko Peleshi (who later became Deputy Prime Minister) in 2009. The central premise was for a 'Patchwork Strategy' of interventions mixing existing and new buildings within areas identified as having potential as 'Development Islands'. These are intended to stimulate economic growth as well as strengthen the cultural and social infrastructure by repairing the urban morphology damaged by large-scale communist interventions.[38]

The scale of the city, which sits to the south of Tirana, is significant. With a population of around 75,000, Korça is relatively small. The practice has been able to gradually win the trust of local politicians to the point where they have executed a series of buildings dispersed around the city that one might consider together as a form of urban polychromy. Colour is not an afterthought; it is in the forefront of most of the projects, as it has been since the earliest days of the practice. In Albania, with extremely limited budgets and a desire to make a difference quickly and overtly, a coat of paint has become a way of establishing and signalling change. The practice had already made a number of projects using a painterly approach on the bland facades in Tirana, perhaps the most memorable being their *Virtual Air Conditioning Units* project. The scale of the painting is immense, taking up the whole eight-storey facade.[39] The colour combination was deliberately dynamic and must have been shocking when first executed. Vivid red and orange stripes with white rectangles irregularly distributed across the surfaces mimic the peppering of air conditioning units throughout the city – camouflaging the real ones among the

virtual. Edi Rama's colourful re-dressing of the city has been so successful that it has become somewhat of a tourist destination – particularly with 'Instagrammable' images grabbing immediate attention on an international stage. Clearly, much of this would not be considered appropriate in most cities. That was never the intention. Rama, himself an artist, seized an opportunity and Albania became a testing ground for the instant fix provided by a simple coat of paint to signify a rejection of the greyness of its recent communist past. Wilson notes that the vivid colours used in Tirana, made with strong colours and cheap paint, fade very quickly in the intense Mediterranean sun. This has come from experience even in northern Europe. The fugitive, unstable nature of saturated external colour can be an issue and will require maintenance, unless a high-quality mineral paint is used. Traditional limewash has always required regular repainting, and red-based pigments are particularly susceptible to degradation in sunlight. More durable materials – such as the deep blue glazed bricks used by the practice at the Münster Library (1987–93) alongside copper cladding – were beyond the budgets available for Albania. Wilson is aware of the temporal nature of this quick-fix approach, noting it as a form of 'pimping'. This sounds derogatory, but it is a common association with paint – that it can be transformational despite its comparatively low cost.

In Korça, the colour is also used to shift the identity at the scale of the city, re-dressing and representing the past. Alongside the simple re-coating, the city has invested in high-quality ground surfaces for parks, traditional stone walls, benches and urban furniture. The practice has woven these new insertions through the city underfoot and overhead, creating places to sit and shelter from the sun, to talk and to stroll. The use of saturated colour at intervals then seems to add a further, more playful and whimsical layer of identity. For example, the *Blue Half-House* (fig.3.23) anchors the corner of a small public space. The house was originally scheduled for demolition as it had been constructed by its owner without permission, but Bolles+Wilson argued for it to be partially retained, slicing off the rear of the house to accommodate the road, but insisting that

3.23   Bolles+Wilson Architects, *The Blue Half-House*, Korça, Albania, 2016

it be painted in blue.[40] The saturated blue is an alien colour in the predominately yellow and red ochres of its surroundings, and it has subsequently become a landmark. More controversially, a tall campanile, now a public outlook tower, was proposed directly on the main axis to the cathedral, offering views of the city and the mountains beyond. It is defined by colour, both in appearance and by name: the *Red Bar in the Sky*, which is carved at the top of the solid concrete structure that is painted white, with one dark grey facade. Recent buildings have used brown tones. A deep purplish brown on the Palazzo Romeo (2019) – similar to the caput mortuum of the Thorvaldsen Museum in Copenhagen – pierced with striking circular openings, a mid-earthy brown on a new

hotel and the brown and white undulating facade of the new Korça City Library (2018) (fig.3.24). Wilson refers to these colours as seeking out 'the depth and poetic resonance of wet earth'.[41]

The external polychromy in Korça tends to be constructed through predominately monochromatic interventions, such as the blue house, the brown library, the pinkish-red facade of a renovated theatre adjacent to the tower, which is spotted with pottery theatrical masks. Occasionally a bright pink is added to enliven an otherwise dull existing facade, where it forms a backdrop to a park space. The colour is a signifier of change, as well as a visual marker of place. In Korça, the spatial painting is at the scale of the city surveyed optically, glimpsed as a progression of successive

3.24   Bolles+Wilson Architects, City Library, Korça, Albania, 2018

of life, moments of pause in the practice's work are accompanied by inflections of colour, either as painted scenery on the enclosing walls or from the use of local materials, stone, copper and timber. Colour is therefore used sparingly, but with intent. The urban polychromy has been cumulative in nature, not pre-scripted. Wilson refers to the use of colour in Albania as 'radical polychromy', picking up on the deliberate politicising of colour by Rama as an instrument to shift the identity of Tirana.[43] Some of the colours chosen can also be considered as radical in that they depart from traditional norms. These moments become nodes (in terms of Lynch's spatial memories), glimpsed in the distance, peeking around a corner and beckoning forward. Although not fully preconceived, the colour can be seen as supportive of the original masterplan competition defined as 'Scenographic Urbanism'.[44] This continues to be an extraordinary method of realisation of a carefully choreographed series of projects and small public spaces within the existing urban grain.

Bolles+Wilson's colour strategy in Korça also extends to building interiors. In the two examples that follow, the first adopts an orchestrated sequence of room to room, while the second is truly polychromatic, juxtaposing different colours adjacent to each other.

The Museum for Medieval Art on Bulevardi Fan Noli (referred to as the Icon Museum by the architects) was completed in 2016 as a retrofit project (fig.3.25). The existing frame structure was renovated by a local architectural practice, with Bolles+Wilson commissioned to focus on reconfiguring the inside of the building to accommodate a large collection of religious paintings that had, remarkably, survived the communist era and were to be shown to the public in the new gallery. The building needed a clear division between 'front of house' and 'back of house' to allow for restoration and archival work to continue alongside public access to the collection. Approaching the museum over a moat, the external appearance was adjusted by Bolles+Wilson by applying panels of matt black over the grey stone, at the request of Prime Minister Rama, who took an interest in the projects in Korça and felt the building resembled a prison. Now, with the rough grey stone and footbridge, the building remains fortress-like,

images. One thinks of Camillo Sitte's plea for an artistic approach to city planning, as opposed to urban design driven by technical or engineering priorities.[42] Sitte drew attention to our appreciation of traditional urban forms, to the irregularity of street junctions and narrowing and widening of the urban fabric, as a series of external rooms. The pedestrian experience of cities has also been highlighted in seminal texts by Kevin Lynch, Hugh Casson and Jan Gehl. These all place human experience at the heart of memorable places, sequences ideally experienced on foot, slowly. Despite its communist past, there was sufficient left of the historical street pattern to allow Bolles+Wilson to make places to pause. In an early interview discussing their projects in Japan, Wilson comments that he prefers to slow down, stop, wait, then move, rather than feeling constantly on the move. Whether a factor of the climate, or a way

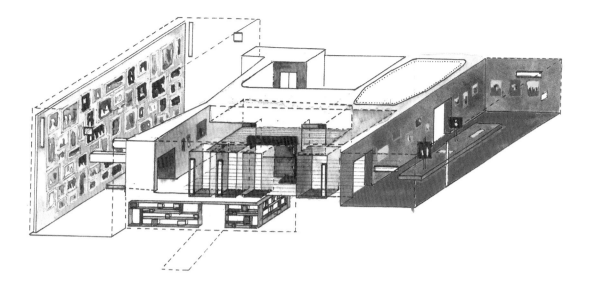

3.25 Bolles+Wilson Architects, Icon Museum, Korça, Albania, isometric drawing showing the sequence of volumes, watercolour

but is perhaps an effective indicator of the treasures housed inside. The public route is prescribed and colour directs the visitor through a linear sequence of spaces, which are ordered museologically and largely determined by the geometries of the existing structure, with an intensely different experience of each space generated through bold colour.[45] Each volume in the sequence is essentially monochrome, but, as at the Schloss Charlottenhof and in the Thorvaldsen Museum, the promenade is orchestrated and the surfaces are painted to create boundaries between rooms, and to evoke strong contrasts when viewing one space from another. In this case there is more interplay of volumes. Entering to the left of reception, the floor was removed to create a double-height gallery. Wilson recounts that this space 'had to be spectacular', and the icon paintings are closely hung against a warm yellow-gold backdrop that wraps on three sides of the space with a matt, black-painted ceiling above (fig.3.26). Although a more obvious choice would have been to use a dark blue or contrast in tone for the background walls, the light reflects very differently from the icons in comparison to the

painting surface, making their gold leaf sparkle. The intention was to create 'an ethereal, transcendental background', shifting the mood of the visitor instantly to reflect on the collection.[46] The intensity and verticality of the picture hang has echoes of the 'Picture Room' at the John Soane Museum in London.

From the gold room, the visitor moves up to the first floor to an open, white-painted balcony, with a shiny white floor, and then into a black and dark grey painted labyrinth with black floor tiles, which is intended to be 'medieval and mysterious'. Small poché spaces off the route are lined in a red-brown wood. From the darkest of rooms, a vermilion red room beckons (fig.3.27), again shifting in volume as well as in colour to accommodate a carved wooden altar screen. The colour is immersive and wraps across every surface, including the ceiling, floor and screens across windows that are masked. The final room in the sequence houses the most precious paintings from the 13th century. They are afforded a focal space and this is executed with pure white walls and an illuminated ceiling (fig.3.28). Peter Wilson's wit is apparent when he notes that this

ABOVE

3.26   Bolles+Wilson Architects,
Icon Museum, Korça, Albania,
interior view

LEFT, AND TOP RIGHT

3.27 and 3.28   Bolles+Wilson
Architects, Icon Museum, Korça,
Albania, interior views

is a reference to Stanley Kubrick's epic film, *2001: A Space Odyssey*, although this reference might be lost on the visitor. Practically, one assumes that the environment must be highly controlled for conservation purposes. A close reading of the colour shows how it is used to imply a particular volumetric technique. The edges between white and black are sharply cut on an external corner. Approaching the white room, the threshold is painted white and the floor extends towards the viewer. Leaving the space, the exit is surrounded by black, with an abrupt line to cross. Similarly, the red extends out into the portal to invite the visitor from the dark grey and black room. There is little visual interplay between the colours themselves as the hue contrast has the most immediate effect, pure red, black, white and gold. Through the simple application of paint and flooring, each surface is identified as belonging to one volume or another. Overall, the use of colour is immersive, intense, and staged as a choreographed sequence. If the architects had adopted a conventional white envelope, without the colour, one would have been aware of the volumetric shifts, but the theatricality of this promenade would have been greatly diminished in terms of how it is experienced.

The most polychromatic interior project to date is the interior renovation of the council offices in Korça, connected by a new underground link to the public 'one stop shop' offices, housed in an adjacent building, which had previously served as the library. They are sited on the main pedestrian axis, Bulevard Shen Gjergi, between the bulbous Orthodox Cathedral to the south-east and a square

LEFT

3.29   Bolles+Wilson Architects, main stair, Mayor's Office renovation, Korça, Albania, 2016

RIGHT

3.30   Bolles+Wilson Architects, 'Radical Polychromy' employed at the Mayor's Office renovation, Korça, Albania, 2016

perpendicular to the travel (fig.3.30). Looking along the vistas, the colours clearly interact with each other, the saturation heightened by the contrast of hue. Wilson remarks that the actual choice of colours makes reference to the Le Corbusier Salubra range and therefore that 'they come pre-balanced'.[47] As previously discussed, however, there was little systematic balance in the Salubra range, nor did Le Corbusier himself use it in any systematic way. There are, however, inherent tendencies to be found here. The main colours used appear to have a similar chromaticness (saturation), and the blue is applied more in shadow and the pink and orange more in the light. The red could be seen to 'fix' the cross-walls in the promenade as it is not positioned in direct light and is thus less likely to leap forward, but rather, adds emphasis to the spatial rhythm. As at the Icon Museum, boundaries between the colours are sharp – made more intensely so by the contrasts in hue (red to green, red to blue, orange to blue and so forth) – and tend to coincide with the corners of walls and junctions. The colour is distributed to accentuate specific surfaces within a spatial setting. As with Le Corbusier, each wall element is unified, but the apparent shape of the space is modified by the colour. In the narrower halls a pale blue and white is used with a lighter tone and a low hue saturation. One reads the plan through the cross-walls and the edges of the portals that interrupt the flow.

So, beyond the restorative and energising effects of a lick of paint, what is the intention of the colour? Is there a deliberate plot by client and architect to somehow make the Mayoral Offices appear more approachable, less formal? It is certainly a memorable promenade. In the adjacent building, also re-configured by the practice, the colour is more conventionally employed, restrained

to the north-east that contains the *Red Bar in the Sky* tower and a newly re-configured theatre, also by Bolles+Wilson. The council offices represent a different form of polychromy, predominately used within circulation spaces in the eclectic 1920s building. The black-and-white tiled floor and simple white ceilings remain, leaving the colour to articulate wall surfaces. There was no possibility to make substantial alterations: instead a 'radical polychromy' is used, bringing non-traditional colour into the inherited rooms. Climbing up the grand central stair, a saturated, cerulean blue wall faces the visitor, made darker in appearance as it is punctuated by a double-height grid of large windows. The stair is flanked with pink-painted walls either side and a white wall at the upper landing. This might appear shocking to the visitor as these are not colours normally associated with authority. The shock is amplified by the portals either side of the stair, which are lined in orange in the thickness of the wall framing a pale turquoise blue beyond (fig.3.29). Along the corridor there are two shades of green modelling a generous octagonal hall, which is then contrasted directly by the vermilion panels on the cross-walls

3.31   Bolles+Wilson Architects, Council Chamber, translucent acoustic walls using
wine bottles set in mortar, Korça, Albania, 2016

to a single wall plane, a ceiling soffit, or an
architectural element, although the choice of colour
remains unexpected – a pink balcony set against
a wall of tightly packed recycled green bottles,
which encloses the public chamber, for example
(fig.3.31). Right at the heart of the city, therefore,
colour is used to infiltrate the everyday workings of
the citizens. It is unusual for a single architectural
practice to be afforded the opportunity to leave
such a distinctive mark on a place. One thinks of
the lifetime of buildings intertwined into the fabric
of Eisenstadt by Karl-Josef Schattner, or by Carlo
Scarpa in Venice. In those cases, the buildings sit
quietly and await discovery. Here, the urgency
of the thirst for change, together with the highly
unusual working method in which colour is an

essential tool, continues to act as a catalyst for
the metamorphosis of the city. Bolles+Wilson refer
to their work as a 'piece by piece choreographing
of the spaces of the historic city centre with
acupuncture-like interventions'.[48]

The palettes of these architects may be
idiosyncratic, but there is a tacit understanding
of the role of colour as spatial modifier. The
projects demonstrate a preference for self-
authored, designed polychromy, rather than
introducing colour through embedded artwork or a
collaboration with an artist. The architects all make
connections between their architectural output
and learning through serial artistic practice, but
crucially for them, they remain in full control of the
composition.

PART II
THE ARTWORK

4.1   Vito Acconci, *The City Inside Us*, MAK Vienna, 1993

4 Pictorial Space

Pictorial space is conventionally defined as an illusion of three-dimensional space and, most significantly, of depth, appearing to recede into the flat surface of a canvas. Where an artwork is embedded within an architectural setting, how does the pictorial space contribute to the bodily engagement of the architecture? How might the concept apply to include a phenomenological space created by colour and light? Having previously discussed the potential for formal tensions between art and architectural surfaces, this chapter will consider spatial depth within and beyond the image through a brief study of murals in antiquity, perspective and illusion, the contribution of dynamic colour fields and contemporary art in architecture. Beyond the spatial effect, how might architecture accommodate autonomous intellectual and social meanings inherent in an artwork?

Artists who intervene within three-dimensional 'found' space have offered extreme re-readings of architecture. Many of these spatial works are temporary, although they may be nevertheless invasive within the space. Vito Acconci's installation, *The City Inside Us*, at the MAK in Vienna in 1993, for example, adopted and replicated the architectural form of the existing main central hall space with its large skylight, reconstructing it in two further iterations, one dropped and one rising out of the ground (fig.4.1).[1] The sloping planes of the artwork altered the actual and familiar space of the hall to present it back to the viewer as a radically new spatial configuration. Gordon Matta-Clark's work in the 1970s, such as his action *Circus (Caribbean Orange)*, made in Chicago in 1978, made cuts through the material fabric of the physical space to create depth by incorporating distant views. The contemporary artist Sarah Oppenheimer's *Project 610-3365* at the Mattress Factory, Pittsburgh (2008) carved through a section of its host building, inserting a plywood construction set at an angle through the floor of a

gallery and out through a window in the wall below (figs 4.2 and 4.3). The altered perspective offers the viewer an unexpected glimpse to the outside, framed within a parquet floor. Unlike Baroque artists who sought to create an illusion of infinite space though 'quadratura' techniques that combined perspective and foreshortening, Oppenheimer re-appropriates the authentic depth of the architecture to heighten the spatial experience of the artwork and also to act as an affective agent in the architecture. Although her work rarely uses applied colour beyond a signature black, it offers an intense and concentrated engagement with architecture through a combination of sensory experiences and cognitive assimilation. Some of her installations are also kinetic and transform the spatial relationships between artwork and architecture through the touch and the push and pull of the viewer.

In advance of creating an installation, Oppenheimer makes multiple drawings, many of them architectural in nature. The logistics of making her artwork require a measured survey and detailed construction drawings. In addition to the precision of these factual studies, she makes digitally modelled drawings that superimpose multiple cones of vision, as seen by a peripatetic viewer. The drawings, extraordinary as projections in themselves, also rehearse the spatial experience of an installation as a series of frozen perspectival moments. When the body moves through an architectural setting, the line of movement may be erratic. For Roderick Lumsden this 'disembodied eye or moving oculus' perceives objects in a different way – not in the same way as viewing from a series of stationary points.[2] These multiple episodic images are clearly more readily captured through film, but Oppenheimer's work, as Julian Rose observes, is 'a carefully calibrated embrace of simultaneity'.[3] Her artwork presents the viewer with a sense of the complexities of human cinematic

4.2 and 4.3   Sarah Oppenheimer, *Project 610-3365*. View from the third and fourth floor.
Plywood and existing architecture. Fourth-floor opening dimensions: 84 × 16 in (213.4 × 40.6 cm),
total dimensions variable. Installation view: Mattress Factory, Pittsburgh, PA, 2008

perception of space. In each of these sculptural examples, the pictorial space – if the term can be applied – and the physical space are intertwined.

Beyond pictorial space constructed through perspective, a fundamental skill of an easel artist is to create a sense of depth on a two-dimensional plane, which may be achieved through the use of colour. In 'Colour and the Arts: Chromatic Perspectives', the philosopher John Kulvicki argues that while 'spatial surrogacy' has been long understood as the distortion of the shape of an object depicted in perspective, there is less awareness of 'chromatic surrogacy' to explain some intuitive skills employed by artists to render complex colour experiences.[4] A simple example given is of atmospheric perception where distant objects appear washed out, the colour being dispersed through the hazy medium of the air. The artist may depict these with lighter tones – the viewer intuits the spatial separation rather than thinking that the actual colour of the landscape is lighter. While we are accustomed, therefore, to an artist making formal adjustments to give an illusion of depth in perspective, the dynamic interaction of hue and tone within the space of a painting is also skilfully applied to manipulate our perception of depth. Paul Cézanne, for example, avoided perspective, relying solely on colour to

4.4　Wall painting on black ground: Egyptianising scene and pair of swans, from the imperial villa at Boscotrecase in the 'Third Style', late 1st century BCE

create depth. Alberto Perez-Gomez illustrates the significance of this for architects:

> Cézanne's work is colour, emotion and feelings and the recovery of a primary experience beyond abstract visuality [. . .] He used blocks of flat colour to achieve a new spatial effect of 'flat-depth' and to demonstrate the experience: the enigma of depth as it is given to embodied consciousness. [. . .] It is imperative that we take Cézanne's lesson to heart: that our visual experience of the world is light and its manifestation is colour; this is seldom acknowledged by design practices.[5]

The wall paintings from the Roman villas in Boscoreale and Boscotrecase have been described as secular and almost exclusively decorative. Maxwell Anderson portrays the fresco painters of the time as itinerant artists carrying picture books from which the householder would select a commission. Of the four stylistic periods defined by the art historian August Mau in 1882, the third period – from around 20 BCE to 20 CE – is the most inventive and decorative, with colour block and abstracted patterns. Walls often had a single monochrome colour of black, red or white, with elaborate floral details. The front room of Schinkel's Bath House at Potsdam (1829–40) has a similar technique on the main wall surfaces, inspired by his visit to Pompeii around 1804 (fig.3.7). In these cases, pictorial depth is experienced predominately using hue contrasts of figure and ground. The 'Black Room' from the imperial villa at Boscotrecase, built by Agrippa around 20 BCE, is another notable example. The limited colour palette and foreshortening of some of the painted details have a similar abstracted quality to the implied depth of oblique figures seen on Greek vases. There is no attempt to make a realistic perspective; nevertheless, there is still a pictorial depth using a profile or flattened frontal view (fig.4.4).

Earlier styles of Roman wall paintings in the first and second periods would conjure up complex three-dimensional scenes with simulated stone and marbling. Figurative and perspectival views made direct allusion to an imagined space beyond the wall, framed with 'architectural confections' of painted balusters or a low wall looking 'out' to a garden or distant view.[6] These virtual scenes immediately conflict with the architecture and the spatial sense of the building when compared with the abstracted images of the third period. The flattening of the picture plane appears to assert the painting as a decorative treatment – not trying to be a painting in the way an easel painting was understood, and not attempting to transport the viewer through the wall into the depth beyond.

The contemporary artist Catrin Huber developed a passion for the Roman wall paintings while working at the British School in Rome. In particular, she was interested in making connections with the use of perspective to bodily engagement in the paintings, as well as the use of colour. A wall painting, *Hall of Fictional Space* (2011) in the British School at Rome, sought to imply a perspectival depth using the most minimal of means. The intention in her work is to activate the viewers, to make them look again, be curious and notice the oscillating experience from different angles of view.

For a permanent artwork in a domestic hallway in Whitley Bay in the north of England (2019), angular forms in vivid yellow, deep pink, blue, silver and pink pick up references to the physical environment, but also to the sunlight and shadow that floods the hall in its coastal location (fig.4.5).[7] The pictorial space changes constantly with the light conditions and reflections in an adjacent glass door, as well as through the anamorphic movement of the viewer in this transition space. An earlier, temporary installation, *Grammar of Clouds* at Sir John Soane's home at Pitzhanger Manor, London (2012), had explored colour and imagined space beyond the surface. In selecting a setting, Huber noted Soane's use of the ceiling in several rooms. In one, a painted oculus suggests that the sky is seeping into the room. Combined with his use of convex mirrors, there is a complexity and tension in the constant play of illusion, supplemented by colour. Huber was drawn to a room that had no ceiling embellishment. Here she used image projections onto the ceiling, of a slit surrounded by cloud forms, reminiscent of the depth revealed in Lucio Fontana's (1899–1968) sliced canvases. Rather than depict an azure sky, the colour of the projection cycled through a series of 12 variations in colour and cloud formations, causing radical shifts in the experience of the room, through the reflected

colour (fig.4.6). Working within these extraordinary historical spaces, Huber's work demonstrates a view of space as more than physical. It is clearly allegorical. For Huber pictorial space is social, cultural, and political, as well as psychological and imagined. The space is charged with meaning, revealed through the use of colour, which draws out social and cultural ambiguity overlaid on the intellectual reading of a physical encounter.

Huber is also influenced by the Russian avant-garde artist and architect El Lissitzky, particularly his small exhibition room, *Kabinett der Abstrakten* (1928), which was unsettling in terms of its spatial properties, distortion and potential for multiple readings. She also refers to his celebrated 'Proun' series of paintings that was extended to the scale of a room installation in 1923. In her writing, Huber concocts fictional conversations between people otherwise separated by history, such as El Lissitzky, the German artist Kurt Schwitters, an unknown female Roman wall painter and herself. They challenge each other to explain their intentions and in doing so, reveal Huber's interpretation of their work and offer a reading of her own practice.[8] Much of the conversation relates to spatial manipulation and the relationship between imagined (painted) and physical space. A series of temporary installations – *Kiosk of Fictional Space* (2010) in Herford, Germany and *As Above So Below* for the Hatton Gallery in Newcastle upon Tyne (2013) – have continued these large-scale works. The Hatton Gallery installation allowed her an exceptional opportunity to set her painting directly surrounding Kurt Schwitters' *Merz Barn Wall* (1947), relocated there in 1966 from its original setting and simultaneously dislocated. In 2018–19, Huber was drawn back to Italy for an extensive collaborative project. She gathered an interdisciplinary team of archaeologists and researchers, focusing on two Roman houses at Herculaneum and Pompeii. Huber's site-responsive artworks, *Expanded Interiors*, although temporary, sought to draw attention to the spatial manipulation, rhythm and irregularity, figures and artefacts and reveal some of the idiosyncratic relationships between the original wall paintings and the architecture (fig.4.7). The project also explored the intersubjective space between disciplines as different interpretations emerged within the collaboration. In both form and in her intensely saturated colours (red, black, yellow, blue, green, pink, purple and white), the intention was to involve the viewer in the physicality of the location, but also to make links to the work of the original wall painters through a use of distorted perspective from multiple viewpoints.[9] In her case, therefore, the focus was on both perspective and the dynamic interaction of hues.

In these examples by Catrin Huber, the abstraction in geometry and the application of flat planes of colour seem to be relatively easily accommodated within an architectural setting. In his book *The Birth and Rebirth of Pictorial Space*, John White offers a further reading of the relationship between the painted Roman walls and the actual space in which they were situated. He argues that the successful examples were not only about the choice of colour, but that the artist also appears to have taken cognisance of the shape and proportion of the room, and the direction of the daylight within the space. Catrin Huber recorded a subtle adjustment made by the Roman wall painters at the House of the Cryptoporticus, Pompeii, to vary the rhythm of their painted columns to take account of an irregular spacing of the windows opposite the wall and form a dynamic composition. Thus, the real environmental conditions – at least those of a frozen moment – would be synthesised into the painted image. John White cites the example of Room 6 in Villa of the Mysteries, a long narrow space lit only from windows at one end where 'the painted architectural features run towards a single centre situated two thirds of the way toward the inner wall. No matter in what direction the spectator at this point may turn, the spatial logic is maintained.'[10] In examples in which the pictorial and spatial readings are at odds, it is often because the viewer cannot achieve the hypothetical position at which the visual and spatial logic is in harmony. The 20th-century mural artist Hans Feibusch made a similar observation: 'this new conception of the mural at once threw up some serious problems that had not existed before . . . the painted architecture easily clashed with that of the real room' and 'required the viewer to stand on a particular axis'.[11] He cites Mantegna's painting in the Eremitani Chapel, Padua, as an example of an awkward spatial relationship, which might have been solved had the artist created an imaginary eye level higher up the

OVERLEAF

4.7   Catrin Huber, *Expanded Interiors*, paintings installed at the Villa Cryptoporticus, Pompeii, 2018–19

wall. In terms of depth, he notes that 'the depth of the picture had to be proportional to that of the room; a shallow room could not be extended very far'.[12] White notes a further level of sophistication in the composition in some of the finest Roman examples. He suggests that the artist took account of the position of the viewer encountering the painting in the room, and introduced a form of anamorphic adjustment, thus distorting the painted composition to be more accommodating to the viewer's expectation, as, for example, at the House of the Ara Massima at Pompeii. This echoes Huber's observations of the dynamic effect of such subtle adjustments caused by using multiple perspectival viewpoints in a single wall painting.

For Feibusch, writing in the mid-20th century, the most successful period of wall painting was the Baroque, particularly through the work of Tiepolo who would marry near and distant views to open up the wall or ceiling, with his painting composed in such a way that the pictorial space felt cohesive with the architectural reality. When it worked, the art and architecture became mutually supportive in an existential ambition to create the impression of infinite space: 'We have here, for the first time, an architectural style not only willing to bear painting as an ornament or help for specific purposes, but needing it out of an innermost necessity, an inability to fulfil itself alone without the assistance of an illusionist's art.'[13]

Feibusch observed that the architecture of his own time – the mid-20th century – exhibited an 'unnecessary rawness' and that there was a place for the architecturally sensitive wall painting to re-emerge. As he foresaw, the 1950s and 1960s were a fertile period in the making of embedded art and large-scale paintings in architectural settings. The process of abstraction, of non-figurative art, perhaps reduced some of the potential conflict between the pictorial space of the art and the real space of the architecture. Colour also became even more significant. It would be folly, however, to try to summarise the multiple threads of artistic production of this period for the purposes of this book; the sense of depth both inside the artwork and beyond the surface is significant. Among the artists of this period who made significant work for specific spatial settings are Victor Pasmore, Patrick Heron, Sol LeWitt, Mark Rothko and Yves Klein.[14]

Discussing pictorial space in abstract art, the art critic Clement Greenberg lamented that art had reached a point where 'pictorial space has lost its "inside" and become all "outside"', and that 'this spatial illusion, or rather the sense of it, is what we may miss even more than we do the images that used to fill it'.[15] His argument is that there was little sense of figure and ground, and that the depth within the image had become shallower – essentially compressed into a flat surface of colour. Without a pictorial scene, how would the spectator escape from their actual surrounding into the space of the image? Greenberg went on to suggest that in abstract art, there was a loss of complexity in the visual language – perhaps even the syntax of that language – previously understood within figurative painting. Hence the eye moves across the expansive field of the painting without having a specific focus, or with a multiple of overlapping points of interest made by the texture and colour alone. The effect of colour and form had become an optical space rather than a pictorial space.[16] Despite his concerns, in terms of the effect of the artwork in the architectural setting, however, this lack of perspectival view seems to present a more accommodating, affective relationship through dynamic sensations generated by colour and light.

In contrast to this sense of a shallow field, Yves Klein's massive colour field paintings at the Gelsenkirchen Musiktheater (1959) sought to transcend the physical and lead the viewer into a form of reverie engendered purely by saturated colour and light (fig.4.8). The background to the commission is notable. His partner, Bernadette Allain, was an architect who helped secure the commission, as well as working on site with Klein. Werner Ruhnau, the architect for the building, had met Klein in 1957, but in an interview with François Perrin in 2003, he recounted that it was Allain who 'instantly knew what I was looking for'.[17] The massive murals were made directly on site, with different techniques used on the main 'solid' wall painting and the side panels. The full width mural was built up in layers of plaster laid on undulating lath; then the monochrome blue pigment was superimposed on this folded landscape. For the side walls, pre-cut sponges of various rounded shapes were dipped in pigment from a wheelbarrow on site and mechanically fixed to the wall surface. In the case

4.8   Yves Klein (with Bernadette Allain), blue sponge relief paintings, 1959,
at the Gelsenkirchen Musiktheater

of these paintings there is a literal depth within the artwork, and within the shadows cast across the surface made by the rough and bulbous textures, but Klein's aim was to draw the viewer deep into the pictorial space using the colour of the blue itself.

Although Klein referred to the influence of Mondrian, Delacroix and Malevich on his work, the passion for ultramarine blue seems to have been triggered by a visit to Giotto's frescoes at the Basilica of St Francis in Assisi. There, the deep blue vault evokes an infinite cloudless sky. Giotto made an even clearer statement at the barrel vault of the Scrovegni (Arena) Chapel (1305) (fig.2.1), where there is almost no embellishment to the pure blue pigment, only gold stars. It is possible that Karl Friedrich Schinkel also visited the chapel on his Italian tour, as he repeatedly used the motif of gold stars on a deep blue background. Yves Klein

recounts his encounter with the deep blue: 'it was therefore indeed through colour that I became acquainted with the immaterial'.[18] Editing all colour down to a single, monochrome composition was also a solution born out of his reaction to an earlier solo exhibition in 1956 where a series of his monochrome canvases (of varied base hues: green, red and so forth) had been hung in the same space. He observed that the audience could not focus on one painting but would inevitably begin to construct imagined hierarchies between the colours, and in doing so, would lose the pictorial intent of each autonomous painting. Klein's singular focus on blue was not only about the sensory experience of the colour but also tapped into cultural meaning and therefore into an intellectual association of the colour. As explained by psychologists, colour is experienced by a combination of 'bottom up' and

4.9   Yves Klein, *Relief Éponge/Bleu RE 17*, 1960, NMSK 1971, International Klein Blue, gravel and sponge on panel, 230 × 153 × 15 cm (90 ⁹⁄₁₆ × 60 ¼ × 5 ⅞ in), Gallery of Modern Art, Stockholm

artworks have been created as artefacts, they are experienced as phenomena – the blue occupies the space and any memory of the building will be intertwined with the memory of the colour. In these paintings, there is a depth of pictorial space – without dimension. Simultaneously, the colour, as light, radiates from the surface into the atmosphere, infecting the air. Hence the pictorial space can be considered three-dimensionally (fig.4.9).

In the case of Klein, the hue and the saturation of the pigment was paramount. As noted in Chapter 3, discussion of colour often suffers from a sloppiness in the use of the word itself. We talk of 'colour', frequently meaning hue (red, orange, etc.); yet the spatial effects of the tone (related to whiteness/blackness and the light reflectance value) and the saturation (chromaticness/intensity) may be more significant than hue in a three-dimensional setting. Like 'chiaroscuro' in drawing and painting, in architecture the tone of any surface will be more significant to the experience of depth, the differentiation of figure to ground, boundaries and the definition of thresholds than the choice of hue – even more so when accentuated by daylight. Artists such as Bridget Riley and Gerhard Richter spent several years simply mastering tone, limiting themselves to black, white or grey tones before introducing the additional plasticity of hue. Similarly, as noted previously, Le Corbusier initially made monochrome easel paintings to study the effect of light and shade, before repeating the study in colour. In traditional Chinese landscape painting, foreground and background are determined by tonal contrast, with the middle distance sometimes being deliberately left unpainted or ghostly pale as part of the narrative. Pictorial depth through tonal manipulation can therefore add a further dimension to the experience of architectural space.

Mark Rothko's murals for the Seagram building (1958–9) were originally conceived for the Four Seasons restaurant on the ground floor of the Mies van der Rohe/Philip Johnson building in New York, and some are now housed at the Tate Gallery in London. They provide a further example of the use of unconstrained colour to evoke pictorial depth and expansiveness predominately through shifts in tone. In common with other artists of the period, these abstract paintings use colour dispersed across the canvas without depiction of a specific

'top down' processing. Reflected light of different wavelengths from a surface enters the eye and is experienced as colour. The cognitive interpretation is then dependent on social and cultural norms and individual memories. It is therefore contingent in every way. Blue alone, according to Klein, carries an association with sea and sky – less tangible than objects. As Gaston Bachelard observed: 'the blue sky, mediated upon by the material imagination, is pure feeling; it is emotionality without object'; and he continues, 'there is an imaginary beyond, a pure beyond, one without a within. First there is *nothing*, then there is a *deep* nothing, then there is a blue *depth*.'[19] The sensation of infinite space is presented to us as a psychological space, which Klein considered as universally understood. At Gelsenkirchen, Klein's vast paintings are absolutely at one with the architecture. While the

form, but with compositional structure through the application of translucency and opacity. The deep red-browns, burgundy, plum and black are tonally different, even if the hues are similar, providing light and darkness that gives the surface a sense of depth. Without a pictorial representation of perspective, the flatness suggests an immeasurable horizon. An initial awareness of the flat surface may, on longer observation, give way to a feeling of a space beyond. It takes an extended visual engagement with the painting to experience this sensation.

The location originally intended for the murals was a small dining room off the main restaurant, but as has been recounted in countless subsequent accounts, they were never hung there. Rothko reputedly walked away from the prestigious commission at a late stage after making around 30 paintings, from which he would select seven for the space. The constrained dimensions of the space seem to have been less significant for the artist than the fact that they would be background art for wealthy diners with little time or interest in looking at the paintings. We can only speculate on the spatial relations and effect of the paintings as no definite arrangement or selection was ever confirmed. The Rothko Room at the Tate provides the closest to a lasting environment. It is an immersive experience in a gallery setting, where, unlike the restaurant, there is no competition for attention. Clearly, Rothko could not come to terms with the conflicted situation and the lack of focus on the artwork that he felt was necessary. The art needed to be autonomous to allow its effect to be felt independently from the contingency of its context.

This seems to be a critical issue. If an artwork is self-sufficient, how is this accommodated within an architectural setting without compromising both? Michael Schreyach makes a useful contribution to the theme of autonomy, meaning and experience in discussing Jackson Pollock's *Mural* (1947). He refers to the art critic Anton Ehrenzweig's controversial suggestion that the experience of the viewer is the meaning of the artwork, whereas Schreyach suggests the aim is to 'distinguish pictorial meaning from actual or literal experience'.[20] The painting being discussed was on a massive scale. It was designed for a specific wall in the town house of Peggy Guggenheim in New York and was one of only two commissions by the

artist for an architectural setting. Nevertheless, Schreyach argues that Pollock's *Mural* – despite its title – succeeded in establishing an independence both from its setting 'and from the contingent experiences of its viewers'.[21] The essay argues that it achieves this separation through the composition itself, the movement of the brushwork and the disposition of the colour across the surface. Pollock's paintings are so immersive that they engulf the viewer. The pictorial space extends inside and outside of the surface to the point that it is described as more of an 'environment', with the viewer as an active participant in the space. The viewer has a bodily engagement with any visual artwork, with the somatic eye darting across the surface drawn by the variety in tone, hue and composition. At the large scale, more common in architectural settings, the whole body is more likely to shift in position, to stand back or to view from multiple angles. Schreyach offers a further analysis on the *Mural*, considering how it would have been experienced in its intended domestic setting. The viewer would have approached the painting at an acute angle but would then feel compelled to move to face the painting in a more conventional face-on view. Pollock overlaid paint with different surface reflectance (satin and matt) so that the light would be dynamic as one moved around the room, which would also elicit movement.

The framing of the work is also likely to be a contributory factor in the way the artwork is perceived and the extent to which the pictorial space of the artwork merges with the architectural setting. As we saw in Chapter 2, there may be tensions between the architectural container and a painting that is directly applied to a wall or ceiling. A framed painting will isolate the image from the wall surface. A wall or ceiling painting made directly on the surface needs to negotiate a position with the spatial setting and will present an artist with a very different challenge – whether purposefully to remain autonomous, or whether to find a way to engage its audience and its setting in a dialogue. We have an expectation of meaning that may or may not be explicit in the artwork, however, as the Swedish poet Gunnar Ekelöf observed: 'in the practice of any art, it is good to leave some space at the table for the reader, the listener, the viewer – and for that space to be made their own'.[22]

5.1   Eileen Gray, 'Untitled', c.1930, gouache and collage on paper, 36 × 32.7 cm
(14 ³⁄₁₆ × 12 ⁷⁄₈ in). Collection Peter Adam

5   Ethereal Material

Material practice is fundamental to both art and architecture but involves very different processes. Unlike architects, who are generally one step removed from physical making, most artists have a direct physical engagement with their work. Artists make, and, in making, they develop a heightened understanding of the material. For painters, this is first and foremost through pigments and paint. Through making, artists develop a palpable understanding of colour, technically and materially.

The way in which we 'see' colour as being inherently part of a material surface is deceptive. Colour is often considered to be somehow embedded within a material, yet once the relationship between colour and light is grasped, the fluctuations in the appearance of colour with changing light conditions are readily understood. Artworks that are intended to be permanently sited within architecture will be subject to very different vulnerabilities than those consigned to a gallery setting and may allow the artist to explore more durable materials. The artist also has the opportunity to observe the situation and to respond to changing light conditions. This chapter will give context to the notion of colour as an ethereal, ambiguous, temporal phenomenon that is part of a dynamic experience of material surface.

AMBIGUITY AND COMPLEXITY – HUMAN EXPERIENCE OF MATERIALITY

The Irish architect and designer Eileen Gray (1878– 1976) came to architecture through art practice. She studied at the Slade School of Art in London and first became fascinated by the craft of lacquering. She is best known for the house *E.1027* (1929) in the South of France, but she also completed several other architectural projects across her long lifetime.[1] She kept notebooks of the lacquer recipes, learnt and practised her technique, and experimented with application and process. In a detailed account of Gray's practice, Rachel Siobhan Tyler notes that the intelligent use and application of colour in her work is not well represented in publications.[2] This is partly because of the lack of contemporaneous colour photography and reproduction, but also because Gray did not feel a need to articulate her work to a wider audience through writing. Finally, as recounted by Beatriz Colomina and others, her significance was diminished because of her gender in a profession that was (and continues to be) male-dominated.[3]

One of the most striking observations to emerge from recent research is the subtle experience of material surface that Gray achieved, which simply cannot be reproduced – even now. Although we may know her furniture designs very well as they are available as reproductions, it was the combination of architectural design, colour, materials, textiles and furniture which would have been experienced in a fully integrated design that is significant. In their book *Eileen Gray: The Private Painter*, Peter Adam and Andrew Lambirth discuss the paintings that she made throughout her lifetime, which she guarded for the most part as a private endeavour. The artwork is clear evidence of her mixing and overlaying of media, abrading the surface, and layering gouache over wax, oil and collaged card with little demarcation (fig.5.1). This ability to work in an artistic process, rather than 'a strategy of settled expectation', gives the paintings a visual and dynamic heterogeneity.[4] Her lacquer surfaces are similarly variegated to reflect light in ambiguous and complex ways, giving a richness to the colour that is obliterated when replicated in reproductions. She also developed skills with dyes for weaving and rug-making that are not only about haptic texture and formal design, but in which the making of the colour is part of the process and the product.[5] Tyler's study of Gray's notebooks reveals a careful documentation of making through experiential

5.2 Eileen Gray, *House E1027*, France, 1929, black gloss tiles and matt wall using layered pigments

subtlety of material understanding. Even looking at the shade of white, there is a depth and liveliness in the way in which the calcium, in a lime-based paint, reflects light as opposed to scattering it. Trautwein notes that the houses predate the introduction of commercial white emulsion based on titanium dioxide, so this was not necessarily of her own making, but the choices of colours and materials certainly were. She also understood the concept of patina and of the quality of a dull surface against a shiny one, an uneven surface against a smooth one, creating 'an irresistible irregularity'.[6] The beauty in her work, which is now being appreciated, is in the sensual contrast of one material against the next, and the relationship of the colours inside the house to the seaside landscape outside, so that by brushing past a blue-glazed surface one is immediately connected to the ocean beyond (fig.5.2).[7]

MATERIAL PRACTICE AND AUTHENTICITY

In conventional contemporary architectural practice, decisions on materials are made in advance as part of the design development and communicated through construction drawings and specifications. Advances in computer-aided design (CAD) rendering and virtual reality environments provide clients with photo-realistic images, where light and shadow can be modelled and animated. In terms of formal design, planning and decision-making, these are now invaluable tools. Except in expensively produced renders, however, the virtual representation of material surfaces remains rather crude in appearance, and most everyday architectural tools are not yet at the level of immersive game design, where gravity, rain, wind, sounds and other environmental conditions are replicated algorithmically and never the same twice. The best of contemporary video games offer a sublime and esoteric experience, but game development involves many hundreds of animators, sound designers, artists, architects and other creative designers over and above the data coders and game designers – all united in an international collaborative practice. In real life, the complexity, contingency and authenticity of human

practice. The furniture had a particular crafting of layers of lacquer, hand-ground pigments and a visual complexity, with one layer shimmering beneath another, which becomes impoverished when translated into contemporary manufactured copies.

In research undertaken by Katrin Trautwein of the Swiss paint producer kt.COLOR, the paint colours used on the walls of her *E.1027* house have been documented and reveal a further depth and sensory experience – of touch, sound, feel, smell and sight – all become embedded in our memories and contribute to a sense of place. Material practice is absolutely central to these experiences of architecture; however, the colour of material surface is processed intellectually in a slightly different way.

Although all colour is light, a surface colour is experienced as a product of the physical material. It seems interesting that our minds somehow interpret the colour of exposed material surfaces differently to an applied painted surface. This split is expressed by the architect Rem Koolhaas: 'there are two kinds of colours. The ones that are integral to a material, or a substance – they cannot be changed – and the ones that are artificial, that can be applied and that transform the appearance of things. The difference between colour and paint.'[8] Koolhaas echoes a similar observation to that made by the philosopher Ludwig Wittgenstein in *Remarks on Colour* where he observed that 'there seem to be what we call "colours of surfaces" and "colours of substances"'.[9] There is immediately an impression that one is more authentic that the other. A similar thread runs through the Austrian architect Adolf Loos's essay *Ornament and Crime*, which argues for the veracity of each material to be displayed for its specific properties, including paint expressed as paint.

Taking an example from sculpture, one is immediately confronted by the scale and texture of Richard Serra's steel sculptures, which celebrate their very steeliness (fig.5.3). Looking closely, we see red-brown, pale shimmering blue, yellow, deep browns, grey, charcoal black and burnt orange. If sited externally, the material will continue to change along with the colour as the work ages. A pulverised brick by the artist Naheed Raza (2005), taken out of its normal context and scattered on the floor of a gallery, is revealed as a heap of powdered clay. As the architect John Tuomey has written, 'the beauty of brick comes from its closeness to raw material – portable packs of clay pigment'.[10] We therefore seem to have a different mindset in terms of the colour of complex material surfaces. The colour appears inherent in the material and modified by the way in which it is crafted, and how it is experienced is ambiguous in comparison with a homogenous coat of paint. Material often invites touch – the warmth of wood, a cool marble floor,

5.3   Richard Serra, close-up view of steel sculpture, Gagosian Gallery, London, 2015

and the multiplicity of pattern and texture in the microscopic surfaces can be difficult to categorise or to represent in terms of a single colour, which may explain this difference in the cognitive processing of 'material' colour. How can artwork enrich the experience of a building through its very material existence? What can an artist bring to architecture through material practices that are not normally afforded to the architect?

In a collaboration with RH Partnership Architects and the scientists in the Chemistry of Health Department, University of Cambridge, the ceramic artist Jacob van der Beugel made a series of 240 handmade concrete panels for a 10-metre-long wall of the new building that extends from outside to inside at the main entrance (figs 5.4 and 5.5). Cast materials, including concrete, can, as Adrian Forty has noted, 'be more accurately described as a *process* than as a *material*', and the colour and

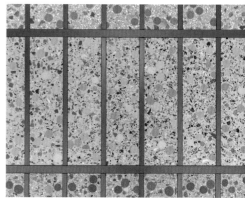

5.4 and 5.5   Jacob van der Beugel, *Matter in Grey*, 2018, RH Partnership Architects, University of Cambridge, Chemistry of Health building

texture are entirely dependent on the recipe of the mix.[11] The aggregate in *Matter in Grey* (2018) is exposed as a polished surface, and the colour varies in each panel to depict the progression of neurodegenerative illness akin to an 'abstracted tissue bank'.[12] The building houses researchers working to understand and combat disorders including Alzheimer's and Parkinson's disease, and the work responds to changes in the colour of brain tissue that are now understood as indicators of the onset of these conditions. Although architects will design in relation to the anticipated tactile qualities and visual appearance of each material, layering, designing and resolving junctions though iterative drawings, architectural design is for the most part a vicarious activity. Architects make drawings and study models, while someone else crafts the object from the materials specified. For many lay people, however, it is the craft of architecture that is one of its most enduring qualities. The joy of bringing what only the eye and mind can see into reality through drawings and models, to the point of touch, sight and bodily experience is, for many architects, the most precious activity they can offer. There is a need to find a balance between many competing factors, to prioritise one element over another, to seek simplicity and modesty where appropriate and to be attentive to human experience, which includes colour.

In Hangzhou, a city south of Shanghai, a series of buildings around the China Art Academy Xiangshan campus, by Amateur Architecture Studio (Wang Shu and Lu Wenyu) (2004–7) are constructed to expose each material set one against the other. Colour and texture come from a jigsaw of small pieces, sometimes re-purposed from previous constructions. Although one might not think of this project in terms of colour as there is little that is applied, colour is everywhere: in the constructed landscape and in the built form, and ever-changing with seasons, variations in daylight and weathering over time (figs 5.6 and 5.7). The enduring popularity of Jun'ichirō Tanizaki's evocative book *In Praise of Shadows*, which has been a staple text for generations of western architecture students since its first appearance in English in the late 1970s, is a sign of the level of appreciation for surfaces (and indeed human faces) that show their age, that resonate with past memories. The approach has been particularly successful in projects that need to be robust and easily maintained. In 2011, the artist Martin Creed was commissioned by the Fruitmarket Gallery in Edinburgh to make a new work within the Scotsman Steps – a public stair that connects the Old Town to the railway station below. The stairs, originally built between 1899 and 1902, had fallen into disrepair, had become unpleasant to use and frequently reeked of urine. As the site for an artwork it was not an obvious choice, but in collaboration with architects Haworth Tompkins, Creed's *Work No. 1059* has transformed the entire experience into a joyful polychromatic flight of marble steps. Reminiscent of Gio Ponti's staircases in the Palazzo Bo, Padua (1936–41) and Villa Planchart in Venezuela (1954), the colour comes entirely from the exposed surface of the stone. Martin Creed's artwork sits comfortably within the original structure of stone and glazed brick, and with each step one is made conscious of the climb or descent, looking down to the colour underfoot (fig.5.8). The idea of patina, of non-precious, non-pristine architecture, is a constant theme in Haworth Tompkins architecture.

One can see this at Battersea Arts Centre (2018), where the carbon-charred marks of a fire have been preserved and incorporated into the character of the spaces, and at the London Library (2013), where Creed was invited to create a tiled marble floor for ancillary spaces as part of a major renovation.[13] The technique of using a material-based palette to set new against old is common to many architects working on renovations. Outstanding examples of this strategy are to be found in the work of the Italian architect, Carlo Scarpa, whose work, which is deeply embedded in and around northern Italy, sets new insertions beside aged materials, with moving results.

5.6 and 5.7   Amateur Architecture Studio (Wang Shu and Lu Wenyu), recycled material and rammed earth walls, China Art Academy, Hangzhou, 2004–7

Walmer Yard, a cluster of new dwellings in London, was designed by Peter Salter and realised in collaboration with Fenella Collingridge, together with a host of collaborators and craftspeople.[14] This project is remarkable in its sensual and intensive material-led approach, in which the colour and texture of every surface has been considered and re-considered, made and re-made. Although the material textures are immediately apparent, the dynamic qualities of light and shadow are manipulated with dexterity and enliven the material. The project cannot be considered as in any way common to a conventional architectural process because it took over ten years in the making (and with an exceptional budget), but it demonstrates an

LEFT

5.8   Martin Creed, *Work No. 1059*, 2011, marble (with Haworth Tompkins Architects), The Scotsman Steps, Edinburgh

BELOW

5.9   Walmer Yard, London, unfolded elevational study by Antoni Malinowski, paper collage, c.2006

5.10   Peter Salter (with Fenella Collingridge and Antoni Malinowski), Walmer Yard, London, detail, completed 2018

intertwining of art, craft and architecture in which colour is used in a variety of ways.

Alluding to Tanizaki's book, Jay Merrick has described Peter Salter's architectural work as simultaneously 'a mixture of solid fact and metaphysics . . . of a relationship between allusion and illusion'.[15] Walking around the building, one's attention is arrested by a sudden red glow behind a timber panel, or a purple patch of light moving across a pebbled concrete floor. Reflected colour leaps from one surface to another and one is never entirely sure where the colour originates. Collingridge recalls time spent observing the effects of coloured glass at the Soane Museum while experimenting with interlayers for the red glass, which throws light across ochre clay plaster sourced from Cornwall. Externally, the artist Antoni Malinowski was invited to develop the composition of applied colour on the rendered surfaces of the elevations with a strong red, a softer pinkish-ochre, a darker red ochre and a warm grey (fig.5.9). In places, the pigment was intensified: an iridescent metallic turquoise light scoop grabs light from above, deep into a landlocked room. The colour stops on a defined vertical line or an outer corner, the edge accentuated as a boundary, mostly to draw attention to architectural form while stressing its presence and purpose as a painted surface. For example, a curving

form appears more evident because of its pale blue soffit set against a terracotta-red wall, while colour applied to the ingoes of windows structures the view to restricted private courtyards (fig.5.10). Some surfaces are smooth, some roughly textured. There are moments of polychromatic interaction between painted surfaces and exposed materials – copper, concrete and timber. Even in the use of the concrete, the colour and tone are manipulated, with a darker tone where birch ply shuttering was used, a lighter tone marking a transition to a phenolic plywood cast, then again to smooth soffits produced by lining the moulds in vinyl.

Internally, elliptical bathroom pods are formed with steel sheet, carbonised to a vivid blue-grey on the outside, and enamelled with a saturated painted hue on the inside, in green or red. Indigo coloured lacquer coats the wardrobes, woven willow walls wrap the lower spaces, while chopped straw and clay lines the curious copper scaly 'Yurt' rooms on the skyline. Little in the project is off the shelf and the hand of the maker is invariably expressed in some way or another. As Will Hunter has observed, it is 'a lesson in craft – not only of technique but also of thought – the building is not an assembly of parts or systems, but a handmade artefact, a burnished singularity a decade in the

5.11 and 5.12   Peter Salter (with Fenella Collingridge and Antoni Malinowski), Walmer Yard, London, detail, completed 2018

making'.[16] Projects like this, where the architect can work across scale from furniture and fittings to door handles, kitchen sinks and bottle racks are rare but treasured for their scarcity. The process of designing Walmer Yard is captured in innumerable sketches, studies and construction drawings that are essential in bringing such a haptic, sensual architecture to fruition.[17] Born out of intensive and sustained interactions between architectural designer, painter/designer and an artist/painter, the project bridges art and architecture – or marks a return to the time when both arts were seen as one (figs 5.11 and 5.12).

DURABILITY

Perhaps because of this emotional attachment to 'real' materials, many architects are reluctant to cover a material with an additional decorative layer. Unadorned materials have a sense of authenticity, and the lack of any coating that will decay or loosen due to weathering and use provides an inherent robustness. The colour of 'natural' materials tends to be a through-colour – such as in brick, stone and wood – not restricted to the surface. However, a layered construction will also improve heat loss and/or gain and can mitigate the effects of weathering and usage. Most architectural surfaces are layered for these reasons. The hierarchy of layers is ever present, so it is what we choose to expose and what to hide that becomes the heart of the question. In considering how colour might be incorporated, the stability and durability of the material is paramount, and this includes artwork that is made for a site-specific installation. Highly stable materials such as ceramic, terrazzo, glass and acrylic polymer compounds will be costly initially but provide exceptional longevity as the pigment is effectively

bound into the material. The surface qualities of these materials that are explicitly handmade or deliberated, smooth and manufactured, also offer artists and architects the scope for variety in texture, reflectance, saturated colour, speckles and imperfections. The appearance of each material will be a product of the processes of its fabrication and is therefore open to manipulation, but also constraints. Collaborations between artists and architects serve to highlight the variance in working practices. Architects conventionally start with a material selection based on performance. For external settings durability is vital, but this can lead to colour decisions based solely on a limited choice of predetermined hue within the chosen product. For artists, particularly painters, there is normally no restriction – they will start directly with colour giving much greater variety and more subtle range of tone, saturation and hue. There are notable exceptions, such as the work of architects Sauerbruch Hutton who are known for their meticulous colour design, often using durable back-painted glass as cladding or as solar control, for example, in an office development at Two New Ludgate in London, 2016 (fig.5.13). Their

5.13   Sauerbruch Hutton Architects, Two New Ludgate, 2016

5.14   Stig Evans, development of colour palette for One Crown Place, London, 2021

confident use of a wide range of subtle tones is unusual and informed by years of research.

A collaboration between artist and architect can have the effect of extending the range and meaning of colour, as well as challenging each party to review and adapt their material practice. In a major high-rise development at One Crown Place in the heart of London, for example, the international architectural practice KPF (Kohn Pedersen Fox) invited artist Stig Evans to collaborate on the development of a palette and composition for the massive canvas provided by the inner facades.[18] The process involved a series of adaptations in material practices from concept, through study paintings, to test panels and final installation. Each stage demanded a translation from one material practice to another through a complex series of collaborative, iterative and empirical processes. Initially, the artist made a series of studies, referring to John Constable's painted skies, which generated small hand-painted samples, with the palette of blues colour-matched to the sky observed at One Crown Place (fig.5.14).

After unsuccessful attempts to match these to standardised colour systems, such as RAL, Natural Colour System (NCS) and Pantone, the solution was to allow a skilled industrial craftsman to replicate the artist's painted colours by eye at the manufacturer's factory, rather than using a coded system. Instead of using fritted glass where the colour is applied on the inside face, the team developed the storey-height panels using a screen-printing technique fired on the outside of the glass, which retained a handmade quality and a softness to the colour tones. The composition retains the concept of the colour as brushstrokes that will vary in appearance with the changing light. The scale of the project is significant in allowing a longer gestation for the 'paintings' to emerge through careful judgement of the placement of each colour prior to their transposition to the facade (fig.5.15).

At the Kaleidoscope building in Farringdon, London, an international collaborative process took place to create the polychromatic facade which has now become emblematic of the building. The result is a clever colour design that reads differently in two directions around the city block using a subtle colour palette of 22 shades in glazed and unglazed terracotta.[19] An established

5.15 KPF Architects/Stig Evans, artist, One Crown Place, London, 2021

5.16   Peter Wood, ceramic artist; tests for flecked glaze, Kaleidoscope, London, 2019

RIGHT

5.17   PLP Architects/Peter Wood, ceramic artist, Kaleidoscope, London, 2019

ceramic artist, Peter Wood (Royce Wood Studio), was invited to collaborate with the architects PLP and the ceramic facade manufacturers to create additional variety in the texture with a hand-applied speckled finish on specific panels (fig.5.16). The intention was to modify the uniformly glazed panels to make a visual connection to the more complex patina of the adjacent copper roofs and ironwork of the nearby Smithfield Market (fig.5.17). In these two projects, it is evident that the approach to colour has been challenged and modified through the collaborative practice.

At Woolwich Arsenal Station on the Docklands Light Railway, London, the artist Michael Craig-Martin was invited to make a large wall artwork, *Streetlife* (2009), for the main circulation space (figs 5.18 and 5.19). One of his signature colours is a vibrant magenta-pink, reminiscent of the Italian fashion designer Elsa Schiaparelli (1890–1973). Having not previously worked in ceramic tiles,

he was unaware that this particular colour would be challenging to achieve in the screen-printed ceramic glaze used in the project. His response was to shift the base colour to a strong greeny-blue, while keeping the same vibrant and highly recognisable colour palette but tweaked to suit the idiosyncrasies of the material production.[20]

In two large commissions for artwork within social spaces in commercial buildings in Germany and Luxembourg, Craig-Martin advised the clients that the investment in using a very durable material – in this case Corian® – would provide an easily maintained surface in highly trafficked spaces. At the HDI-Gerling Assurances offices in Hannover, in the 40-metre-long artwork *The Five Senses* (2010), the background is the vibrant pink that was not achievable with ceramic but works well in the slightly milky, translucent quality of Corian®. In a works cafe space at the European Investment Bank in Luxembourg, the wall 'painting' is 84 metres long and is also manufactured in Corian®. For this project the French manufacturer was asked to develop 10 non-standard colours. Both artworks are inlaid with fine lines that are computer-etched into the surface about 10 mm deep; then, in a process akin to timber marquetry, the material is heated and gently hammered into the grooves to achieve a super-smooth surface. Not only is the colour achievable but the process seems to suit the nature of the artwork. Craig-Martin conceives the works as having a sculptural quality, although the images of everyday objects are deliberately flattened in perspective. The inlay process is also three-dimensional but made to look flat. In the same building, Craig-Martin used different colours of timber inlays to form a second artwork, *Parade* (2008), on the floor of the atrium. Thus, the conceptual basis of the work has a consistency of line art and block colour infill, but the materials of the execution vary to suit the location and the typology of the architectural setting.[21]

At the One Eagle Place office development in Piccadilly, London (2018), the sculptor Richard Deacon was invited to collaborate on a major project with Eric Parry Architects (figs 5.20 and 5.21). Here, the process of manufacture for a massive ceramic frieze was fraught with uncertainty. Numerous prototypes were made by casting with solid colour in pigmented concrete,

5.18 and 5.19 Michael Craig-Martin, *Streetlife*, 2009, screen-printed ceramic tiles, Woolwich Arsenal Station, Docklands Light Railway, London

5.20 and 5.21   Eric
Parry Architects with
sculptor Richard
Deacon, ceramic
facade at One Eagle
Place, Piccadilly,
London, 2018

but the complex geometry and structural weight led to catastrophic failures in the testing process. In further experiments with ceramic materials, the application of a coloured glaze also caused technical failures. The final version uses a floated colour transfer – normally used on small-scale pottery or china tableware – in an apparently random, but highly systematised, sequence of colour and pattern meticulously ordered by Deacon. The undulating profiles of the blocks expose the bare ends of each sectional cut and make it evident that the colour is thinly applied. Seen at an acute angle, the colour on the frieze is less apparent, appearing and retreating in perspective as one moves along the street. The frieze has a somewhat uncomfortable relationship to the more conventional glazed ceramic construction of the rest of the elevation, which includes a blush of pinkish-red at the first-floor level. Parry's stated aim was that the entire facade should stress its artifice, as a thin veil to the structure behind, and be less about an expression of its craft. The glossy surfaces of the facade are intended to reflect the multi-coloured, constantly changing neon lights from Piccadilly Circus nearby and add to the eclectic character of the building. Their aim was to avoid a clash of personalities in the built expression, but the resultant relationship between art and architecture is not without its critics. The process was based on trust, and there was risk at all stages and for everyone involved. Both Parry and Deacon came to the project with experience of the unpredictability inherent in ceramic processes. Deacon's *Fold* sculptures have a beautiful, deep green glaze, but this was considered insufficiently durable for the exterior site. At the Holburne Museum extension in Bath (2011), Parry used cast ceramic cladding with a speckled appearance. It was single-fired and twice-glazed with a first coating of manganese and a sprayed titanium layer that sits beautifully in the dappled shade of the garden setting. The result was a lucky accident of the 'kiln gods' in initial experiments by the ceramists, Darwen Terracotta. At Wimbledon School of Art (2003), Parry had worked with the artist and educator John Mitchell on a facade that used tessellated glazed brickwork in red and blue. The former Dean of Wimbledon School of Art, George Blacklock, reflects that

Mitchell was an 'exceptionally dedicated and persistent artist', adding that he would 'follow the logic of his ideas and methodology through familiar patterns into new territory'.[22] The same comment can be applied to the Piccadilly building process, where artist and architect were never entirely sure where the empirical material practice would lead. The project may not have turned out as anticipated by both parties, but it serves as an antidote to much of the blandness of most current commercial projects.[23]

PAINTING WITH LIGHT

An understanding of the way in which materials reflect and absorb light is fundamental in using colour in architectural work. For example, traditional 'copperas' limewash applied to the exteriors of buildings across Scandinavia (and also found in Scotland), has a vividness emanating from the mineral-based material.[24] When surfaces are seen adjacent to conventional wall coatings, there is a flat dullness to paint and a glowing vibrancy to the pigmented limewash. Although copperas has excellent technical qualities in relation to the breathability of the wall surface, the main drawback is its lack of durability and mottled, uneven and unpredictable appearance, which means that it has substantial maintenance requirements that preclude its use in most circumstances. High-quality, contemporary mineral paints are readily available with similarly good light reflectance and a more even, exceptionally durable appearance. Although still used in restoration projects, traditional pigments are not normally used in conventional architectural practice, given the cost, knowledge and skill required in their application. Yet they offer a reaction to light that is very different from industrial paint.[25]

A central theme in the work of artist Antoni Malinowski is his fascination with light reflectance and pigment. He has executed a substantial number of in situ artworks in collaboration with contemporary architects.[26] Originally from Poland, Malinowski studied at the Academy of Fine Arts, Warsaw and the Chelsea College of Art in London. It was his time spent in Italy, however, as an Abbey

5.22   Antoni Malinowski/Haworth Tompkins Architects, Royal Court Theatre bar, 2000

Scholar at the British School in Rome in 1998 and in Venice in 1999 which is at the root of his interest in the use of historical pigments. Venice was historically the hinge point in the trading of exotic pigments, ranging from lapis lazuli from Afghanistan to carmine red from South America.[27] In common with Goethe, Soane, Schinkel and later, Rothko, Malinowski was fascinated by the Roman wall frescoes and the extraordinary red of the Villa of the Mysteries near Pompeii (60–70 BCE). The intense experience of this red is a consistent thread in his work.

Malinowski's first large-scale project at the Royal Court Theatre in London exemplifies his use of traditional powdered pigments in an extensive wall painting on the outer curve of a drum-shaped wall that wraps the old auditorium and rises up through the renovated theatre (fig.5.22). The project was also the first of several collaborations with the architects Haworth Tompkins.[28] The theatre is located on the east side of Sloane Square in London, and the evening sunlight floods into the foyers, which face the square, anticipating the evening performances. The artwork responds to the sunlight, but also to the movement of car headlights as they negotiate the adjacent streets. The 86-metre-square installation took four months to complete, an extraordinary level of commitment, working in the dust on a building site. The making of the artwork in situ is significant for a number of reasons. First, the opportunity to observe the passage of light when developing the painting (as Tiepolo did in Würzburg), but also to understand and synthesise the way in which the architectural spaces would be used. In some lower sections of the wall painting, the pigment appears lighter, with less dense layers, as though to anticipate and moderate the inevitable scuff marks. The project was completed in 2000 and its robustness has already endured 20 years of use. As theatre director Vikki Heywood notes: 'He's created a work of art that's completely durable. It's not precious – you can walk up to it and touch it and lean against it.

The mapping of the way that the light moves across the wall is fantastic.'[29]

Malinowski had spent several years in advance of the project researching and experimenting with vermilion pigment. In some places there are three or four superimposed layers – patches of light and dark appear to drift across the surface in an ambiguous manner. One is unsure whether they are part of the painting or shadows playing across the surface. The irregularity of the forms seems to be a further factor in the painting's ability to withstand the patina of age and use. A pristine surface would not have been able to accommodate this level of human interaction, through touch in the busy spaces of the foyer and bar, without showing signs of deterioration. As noted in the introduction, in contrast to easel paintings, a painting made by applying pigments directly to an architectural surface becomes part of the space. It is essential to

5.23   Antoni Malinowski/Haworth Tompkins Architects, detail of light and shadow on vermilion wall, Royal Court Theatre, 2000

5.24   Bolles+Wilson Architects, Luxor Theatre, Rotterdam, 2001

5.25   Antoni Malinowski/Bolles+Wilson Architects, Luxor Theatre, Rotterdam, 2001

the architecture and to the atmosphere of the space for which it is made, and subject to a different set of vulnerabilities to a canvas that may be sold on many times, forgotten, lost or damaged. The wall painting embeds the image within the fabric of a building, implying permanence, yet remaining vulnerable to the durability of its container.

Malinowski dislikes emulsion paint and disdains the unthinking use of titanium white which coats the majority of architectural surfaces. It is his deep interest and understanding of the nature of the pigment itself – at a microscopic level – that makes the artwork dynamic and complex. Malinowski has observed the ability of vermilion to appear starkly different, depending on the light: 'in sunlight it appears the brightest of all colours, while in the dark it looks the darkest'.[30]

This extends our understanding of colour in comparison with standard 'off the shelf' paint: it is a metaphysical experience of colour as light. The wall is red, but it is not experienced as red. It will be remembered as red, yet it is experienced as a multitude of different tones (fig.5.23). His large easel paintings have also explored the medium, as noted by the curator of an exhibition of his work at Gimpel Fils, London in 2004: 'in Malinowski's paintings, and in life, colour does not exist so much as happen.'[31]

There is a description of the installation of an extensive wall painting at the Luxor Theatre (fig.5.24), in Rotterdam (designed by architects Bolles+Wilson) in a documented conversation – 'Luxor Letters' – between the architects and the artist.[32] One can easily imagine the artist's daily wanderings around the empty foyer and being suspended 18 metres high on a scaffold while making the painting (fig.5.25). The same vermilion red glaze is used here as at the Royal Court Theatre, alongside carbon black (from soot) overlaid on red emulsion of the vast foyer walls. In this project, the red colour had been integral to the architectural design since the competition stage. A continuously wrapping and rising red wall that follows the ramped and curving journey of the theatre backstage access is mirrored in the

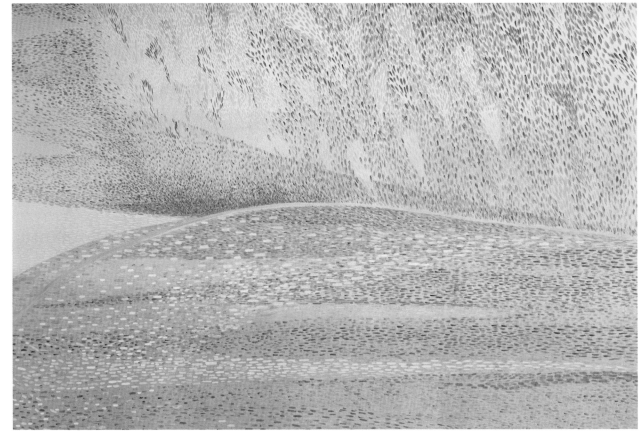

LEFT

5.26 and 5.27   Antoni Malinowski, *Spectral Flip*, 2015
(Rafael Viñoly Architects), Oxford

rising route taken by the public through the foyers. In addition to the large wall painting, a diptych, *Synchrony Carmine*, was hung on the route. Moments of density are made by Malinowski in the painting using tiny drops of deep carmine red (cochineal pigment from crushed beetles), 'a dot with the intensity and presence to balance the remaining 30m² of the total image'.[33] His fascination and understanding of the properties of these rare pigments has developed over time and through use, but also though his early research on Roman pigments. Vermilion is made of mercury and sulphur – a concoction of yellow sulphur and 'quicksilver' – and is very dense, in comparison to carbon black pigment which is light in terms of its relative weight. He enjoys this paradox; black may appear dark, but is light in weight, whereas the red may appear airy and is very heavy. He notes of vermilion: 'its colour is very special, a pure red (neither bluish nor orangey), absorbing all but the red within the spectrum. Vermilion's molecular structure is particularly volatile: occasional electrons can be knocked out . . . causing a change from bright red to black.'[34] It is understandable that he has described the use of real pigments as alchemic. The pigments behave unpredictably so there is a level of risk involved in painting directly in this manner. The result, as was the case with Eileen Gray's work, seems impossible to capture adequately in any photograph. Conventional colour theory also tends to fall short of describing the complexities of surface reflectance, lustre, glossiness, sparkle, iridescence, fluorescence and translucency that have occupied the minds of philosophers as well as artists and architects for centuries.

Having mastered the application of vermilion pigment to reflect light, Malinowski has since undertaken projects that he describes as 'painting out the light', using mica paint as a base. The largest installation to date, *Spectral Flip*, is in the Andrew Wiles building for the Mathematics Institute in Oxford, which was designed by Rafael Viñoly Architects and completed in 2015 (figs 5.26 and 5.27). To understand this painterly process, the following quotation describes how the painting developed as a response to the light on site over a period of three months:

Each day the journey of light is registered on the two large white walls facing each other in the luminous foyer. My work begins by sensitising this background by applying a reflective paint made with mica ground to a fine pigment. Then on the south facing wall, using light absorbing pigments, I paint in colours related to the warm end of the spectrum – from red to yellow. These light wave subtractive earth pigments have been used by painters for around forty thousand years. On the north facing wall, other historical pigments like green earth, lapis lazuli and azurite are going to mark the cool end of the spectrum – from green to violet. An additional layer of brush strokes will be painted with contemporary paint, made with nano technology interference pigments. These don't absorb light but bend the wavelengths. The interaction of these two ways in which colour is 'produced' will create the dynamic of the paintings. The wall paintings will appear very different from different viewing points and with different light conditions. The colour will oscillate between darkness and light, appearing and disappearing, showing different sides of binary complementarities. One elongated thin line in each painting will contribute to the opening of the pictorial space – an invitation for an imaginary spatial journey.[35]

The commissioner for the artwork, Vivien Lovell of Modus Operandi, describes the final result as extraordinary in the way it has altered the experience of the space. Where previously there were two parallel white walls, they appear to dissolve and dissipate colour around the space. Malinowski's painterly practice has developed from this interest in the materiality of both historical and contemporary pigments, with a focus on their specific light-reflectance properties. The advent of new materials such as nano pigments offers artists

5.28 Antoni Malinowski/Haworth Tompkins Architects, stair at Donmar Warehouse office, London, 2014

brightly illuminated shimmering icons, to the fading light and shadows of Titian, to the candlelit scenes of Caravaggio. 'So much of what colour is about is light. The letting out or the holding back of light; luminosity and darkness.'[36] Painters are skilled in the depiction of abstract polarities of light and dark, hue contrasts, attraction and repulsion, proximity and distance. Surrounded by darkness, intense moments of illumination are accentuated. In a logical conclusion to this historical drift, artists have recently adopted technologies initiated by the space industry in order to make use of a material that absorbs 99 per cent of the available light, thus becoming the blackest black currently possible. 'Vantablack' is a coating composed of carbon nanotubes and was originally developed for the inside of optical instruments for use in space. The most extensive use of Vantablack (VBx2) to date was on a temporary pavilion for the Winter Olympics in Pyeongchang, South Korea in 2018, by the architect Asif Khan (in collaboration with the inventors Surrey NanoSystems). The extraordinary structure had slightly concave exterior walls, with small white lights on protruding rods. Scattered with bewilderingly bright white lights and contrasted by an intensely white interior, the experience was reported to be close to a sensation of infinite space. This drive to extinguish all light reflectance has since sparked a race to make the blackest possible black pigment, which saw artist Anish Kapoor reputedly acquire sole rights to Vantablack.[37]

ECSTATIC COLOUR

At this point it may be useful to clarify some of the often perplexing properties of colour and light, and to consider how contemporary artistic practice has continued to evolve its material practices to encompass colour experiences that are beyond conventions of 'subtractive' colour, hue, tone and saturation. One of the joys of colour is its dynamic variability, its ethereal impermanence. In addition to the three colour dimensions of hue, tone and saturation, the experience of colour is also dependent on 'brightness', which is related to both hue and light reflectance. A material with a specific

further opportunities for artwork that explores the way in which colour is experienced beyond the surface. Malinowski's experiments with mica are evident at the *Saturated Staircase* installation in the Donmar Warehouse office, London, a further collaboration with Haworth Tompkins from 2014. Here, vibrant red, pink and ultramarine blue form an underlay, with light-reflective geometrical shapes overpainted and changing with light as one moves on the stair. Each layer of pigment is hidden or revealed to allow the light to interact with the surface. The stair is set slightly off the old brick surface. Although applied as a two-dimensional layer, the painting has a four-dimensional quality as space and time are also factors in the atmosphere that the colour creates (fig.5.28 and cover).

In his book *In Praise of Painting*, Ian McKeever suggests that the history of painting follows a line that successively 'squeezes out the light' – from

chromatic saturation will appear more colourful when illuminated by direct light. An example would be to imagine a yellow taxi: it has a defined hue, a defined tone (or lightness – white to black) and a defined saturation (or chromaticness). When seen on a dull day, the taxi will appear as a saturated yellow, but on a sunny day it will be much brighter, simply because of the intensity of light falling on the surface. A further example of such brilliant colour is when translucent coloured materials are illuminated from within. Mark Fairchild's definition of five modes of viewing colour may be helpful here. A 'surface' colour is equated to the colour of an object (as the product of how much of a particular wavelength of light is reflected and others absorbed); in an 'illuminated' scene a grassy field in sunlight will reflect green light and shadows will be cast; an 'illuminant' – such as a coloured LED light source, or a fluorescent tube wrapped in a gel filter – will be seen to glow; a 'volume' colour is seen as a contained quantity of transparent substance such as red wine in a glass; and finally, a 'film' colour is non-objective, and dispersed, akin to an atmosphere or gaseous medium.[38] So far we have focused on the first two modes in relation to surface conditions.

The artist David Batchelor has invigorated discussion on colour in art and architecture through a series of polemical publications, and through his own material practice. He enjoys the paradox that colour is often considered to be simplistic, yet the complexity of human experience of the metaphysical phenomena continues to be remarkably resistant to analysis. Much of his work has an intense brightness generated by a combination of materials and illumination. Using found objects – such as plastic bottles, sunglasses, watering cans, pipes made of acrylic and plastics – lit with fluorescent tubes or, more recently, LED lights, his colour palette is immediately recognisable. In *Magic Hour* (2004–7), bright pink, red, green, turquoise, yellow and orange boxes are stacked facing directly into a wall, casting intense light on the surface that glows, or facing directly outwards, with the coloured light infecting every surface it meets. The hues and saturation have an affinity with the palette of Michael Craig-Martin, but because they are self-illuminated, they are much brighter. Perhaps because of this intensity,

5.29 David Batchelor, *Chromorama*, 2015, stainless steel, Plexiglas, LEDs, 2100 × 150 × 150 cm (826 ¾ × 59 ¹/₁₆ × 59 ¹/₁₆ in), Broadgate, London

which appears to further increase after dark, the majority of his permanent commissions have been for external sites, such as the neon globe, *Homage to Doctor Mirabilis*, Leiden Square, Oxford (2018), or the 25-metre-tall *Chromorama* (fig.5.29), in Broadgate, London (2015). His luminous colours 'escape their containers and bleed into the street'.[39] One permanent artwork, *Treasure Magic Hour* (2004), is sited internally in a tall niche on the stone stair at the Treasury in London, grabbing visual attention in its subdued surroundings. We experience the work as intensely colourful, not only because of the illumination, but also because of his specific choice of hue. In an academic paper on attention responses to different hues experienced on a digital screen, a group of researchers concluded that in this medium, yellow-green, green and cyan attract the most attention, followed by red and magenta.[40] Batchelor's palette has also homed in on these hues. His work sits in a longer genealogy of 'light' artists such as Daniel Buren and Dan Flavin, and further extended to digital programmed artwork by Jason Bruges, as discussed in the next chapter.

ETHEREAL MATERIAL

Finally, there are a number of 'environmental artists' – notably James Turrell, Ann Veronica Janssens and Olafur Eliasson – whose work engages with colour as an atmospheric 'film'. These are most commonly experienced as temporary immersive installations and, given the ephemeral medium, are less easily accommodated within conventional architectural settings. Eliasson's *Symbiotic Seeing* installation at the Kunsthalle, Zurich, 2020 is an example that took the viewer into a staged event space where the air was infected with colour, moving patterns, refractions and reflections. Turrell has made a number of well-known permanent works that are not reliant on a constructed scenario, but rather they use an oculus to the sky, allowing the viewer to focus on the ever-changing atmospheric colour seen against the fine edges of the aperture. Ann Veronica Janssens is known for her 'mist' rooms that scatter and diffuse coloured light through refraction in the wet environment. In Vienna, a permanent installation by Eliasson for an office building uses the boundary between the pavement and the facade. *Yellow Fog* (2008) appears each evening at dusk, drifting around the legs of pedestrians with an ethereal presence (fig.5.30).[41] Occasionally the wind blows the mist away. These artists are working with colour in its most impermanent and contingent state.

An artwork embedded into architecture may therefore encapsulate the intense physical energy of the maker and introduce a concentration of complex material surface that may be multi-layered, multi-coloured and full of meaning and emotion.

LEFT

5.30   Olafur Eliasson, *Yellow Fog*, 2008, Verbund Headquarters, Am Hof, Vienna

6.1   Tess Jaray, *Minuet*, 1966, oil on canvas, 180 × 228 cm (70 ⅞ × 89 ¾ in), Museums Sheffield

6 The Artist's Perspective

'If you are in the studio, painting, there are no rules other than the rules you set yourself, so you can do anything. And that is the problem.'[1]

The preceding chapters have focused on architects and architecture as a container for artwork. Drawing on a series of interviews, this chapter aims to synthesise earlier themes of surface, siting, scale, pictorial space, colour, light and material practice from the perspective of six contemporary artists who have been commissioned for, or who have collaborated with, architects on permanent artworks in architectural settings. The open-ended and essentially singular nature of artistic practice is deftly captured in the remark by the artist Tess Jaray. How do artists, accustomed to making art that is autonomous, respond to the practical constraints inherent in site-specific architectural commissions?

SINTA TANTRA: CROSS-CULTURAL COLOUR

There has been a noticeable recent surge in the use of applied colour in the urban environment. In her paper, 'Tactical Urbanism: Colour Interventions with Purpose', the Australian academic Zena O'Connor discusses the increased occurrence of urban interventions using highly saturated colour to make claims on space, to redefine territory for the pedestrian, to signify the need for traffic to slow down and so forth.[2] She reflects that the majority of these are short-term, 'pop-up' installations, which are often made by community-based artists but that may become adopted as permanent. Not only do these interventions redefine spatial boundaries within the urban fabric, but the colour has an immediate impact in shifting the impression of a place that may be threatening, underused or

neglected. The renovation of the Superkilen Park in Copenhagen (2012), divided into black and white and vibrant pink areas, is frequently cited as an example of such interventions.[3] Although time, weather and use have impacted on the strong colours, which have faded, their cultural and social sense of place in the city has been secured.

In London, a series of urban works – some commissioned through the agency of the London Festival of Architecture – have become emblematic of a group of multicultural artists and designers based in the city. These include Camille Walala, Yinka Illori, Morag Myerscough, Adam Nathaniel Furman and Sinta Tantra, all of whom are at ease crossing between a wide variety of scales and media. Walala started as a textile designer but is now dressing buildings, lining streets and designing street furniture and jewellery. Illori also works across disciplines and his largest projects to date have included *Happy Street* (an underpass) and the temporary *Colour Palace* pavilion at Dulwich (2019); his studio also designs furnishings and kitchenware. Furman has become established as a leading figure in the resurgence of interest in the use of colour, in the architecture and design of the postmodernist period, and in the heyday of the seminal design practice, Memphis.[4] He has designed rugs, ceramic tiles, placemats, door handles and interiors, and has also worked at a larger scale on a ceramic tile wall installation, *Radiance*, at Chelsea and Westminster Maternity Hospital (2019), and on a series of pedestrian crossings – *Look Down to Look Up* – in Croydon (2018). These joyfully expressive urban works have quickly become memorable as landmarks, and the use of such intense and polychromatic patterns draws attention to the urban site – particularly in the age of social media. These designers are operating between art and design, fusing disciplines, and expanding practice, but approach their work predominately through a design process.

Sinta Tantra (b. 1979) defines herself as a painter and works as an easel artist as well as making large-scale urban paintings and artworks embedded into architectural settings. Her work has a spatial, painterly dimension and her use of colour comes with a fundamental interest in pictorial space. She has worked internationally on vibrant urban installations on ground surfaces, such as the *Temple of Flora* in Hainan, China (2021) and on industrial containers for a floating hospital in Indonesia, *Razzle Dazzle* (2020). Wherever she works she is conscious that 'the first task is to figure out the canvas'. In an architectural setting, this means not only taking the physical setting into account but also the cultural and historical context of the work. The painting emerges in response to the 'canvas'. Her urban painting, *A Beautiful Sunset Mistaken for a Dawn* (2012), at Canary Wharf wraps a two-dimensional pattern around a 300-metre-long bridge, revealing the three-dimensional form. The colours are derived from observation of the water in its docklands site (fig.6.2).

For the Dulwich Picture Gallery in London, Tantra was commissioned to make two large wall paintings that sit facing each other in the entrance hall. The work, *The Grand Tour* (2020), addresses the architecture of Sir John Soane's gallery and his use of arched forms, but also the conceptual idea of colonial cross-cultural appropriation of colour. As noted in Chapter 3, Sir John Soane remains a highly influential figure for many contemporary architects. His use of light, from multiple skylights, animates often intensely crowded rooms. Similarly, colour choices were often exuberant, affirming his love of Pompeian red, green and yellow, which shift in appearance with the daylight. Tantra's wall painting refers to the way in which these imported colours were considered to be exotic. Colours (and rare pigments) observed through travel and brought back into a new context, were used historically as a direct symbol of wealth and, in the 19th century, the consequent ability to travel for leisure and study.

Like many artists, Tantra feels it took time to find her authentic voice and colour was integral to that process. In art school she felt an undercurrent of institutional racism that might be classed as unconscious bias, but which was nonetheless pervasive. As an Asian female artist, there seemed to be certain expectations of the nature of her

6.2 Sinta Tantra, *A Beautiful Sunset Mistaken for a Dawn*, 2012, at Canary Wharf, London

6.3   Sinta Tantra, *The Grand Tour*, 2020, entrance hall, Dulwich Picture Gallery, seen in the context of the John Soane Gallery, London

6.4   Sinta Tantra, *The Grand Tour*, 2020, Dulwich Picture Gallery, London

work. Tantra pushed against this, re-appropriating a dusky pink, although conscious that the colour was immediately considered feminine. The idea of gendered colour seems bizarre, yet colour comes with socially and culturally constructed meaning and associations that can be deeply ingrained. Tantra was born in New York of Balinese parents, but grew up in London. She finds it interesting to fuse colour from her own international and cultural heritage with colours that are associated with 'period' architecture and stately homes, such as Wedgewood blue and gold. Her use of soft turquoise blues, green and pinks is different from the colours often glibly associated with Asian countries, such as the clear oranges, reds and yellows of India. She suggests that the colours of Bali need to be seen in the context of lush green rainforests. Her appropriation of colour, taken out of context, hints at the undercurrent of British colonial plundering that was rife in the 19th century.

Tantra developed her techniques through easel painting, using tempera paint on linen, occasionally leaving glimpses of the canvas bare. She mixes colour to heighten the 'glow' of the pigment with a touch of fluorescent pink or with multiple blues. Conceptually, a similar technique is used at Dulwich, but with industrial paint applied over a white underpainting. The white lifts the colour and shifts the experience of the space dramatically from its previous dark green. The wall paintings have transformed and de-institutionalised the intermediate buffer space between the parkland outside and Soane's intense red picture galleries (fig.6.3). Also, the colours are used to give the impression of pictorial space through adjacency in both tone and hue. She implies transparency through tonal shifts of three blue-greens that appear layered but are not. By placing one tone of the same hue tightly against another, with the edges of the form encompassing both, it appears as though the paint has become see-through. A white semi-circular form is barely distinct from a slightly different tone of white background. Tantra acknowledges an interest in the early 20th-century Bauhaus artists in relation to both colour and form. One sees clearly how some of the techniques demonstrated in Josef Albers' seminal book, *Interaction of Color* (1963), are used here.[5] The geometric forms also produce mutual tensions, just touching here, overlapping there. A fine meandering line is drawn across the forms, taking priority in its apparent planar position. As the line crosses a threshold, it changes from white to black.

Although the forms are flat and appear to adhere to the plane of each wall, colour and form are also in a dialogue across the architectural

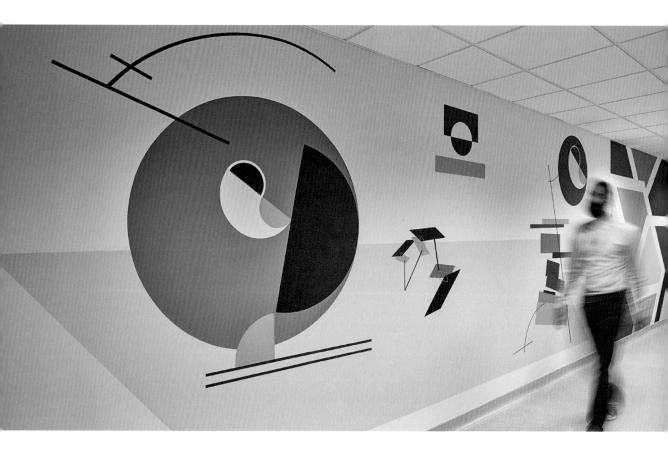

6.5 Sinta Tantra, *The Sound of Colours*, 2017, at the St Paul's Way Medical Centre, London

space between the two parallel paintings. There is a dynamic interaction between the more sombre blue/white/gold on one side and the dusky pink, blue-greens and black opposite. A large circular disc of gold leaf appears to hover, not quite anchored to the surface. Against the other matt forms, the disc catches the changing light from the skylight above. Visitors to the gallery enter between these two paintings (fig.6.4).

In a second, permanent installation – *The Sound of Colours* (2017) at the St Paul's Way Medical Centre in London – the colour and forms used by Tantra vary in relation to the immediate contexts along the length of a wall within the circulation space (fig.6.5). The artwork was conceived to respond to different sensitivities as the visitor

moves through the space or exits from the lift. At one end of the wall painting, wide white lines cross and cling to the wall, subdividing colour blocks into angular forms and leading the eye to postulate spaces above and below. A broad white band appears to lead towards a door. There is no frame other than the boundaries against ceiling tiles and linoleum floor. It is an uneasy composition that does not quite fit the space, similar to the work of artist Michael Craig-Martin, who will deliberately clash painted objects against architectural elements. On the left side, the painting does something entirely different, with a series of objects floating freely against a pale pink backdrop. Tantra describes the two different rhythms as 'dynamic' (to the right) and 'open' (to the left). Her use of colour here is soothing. Her title refers to her continued interest in early 20th-century artists including Wassily Kandinsky. She has clearly accepted Kandinsky's advice to avoid the shrill of yellow, abstaining from a pure triangular form or a pure square, but happily allows a large blue circle to float and expand on a pale pink background, intersected by semi-circles and lines and heaped polygons. In terms of its contribution to the experience of the space in which it is sited, the painting is certainly intriguing. A feeling of unity is achieved through the use of colour. One senses that, in common with her bridge painting, passers-by may stop and wonder what it means and would miss it if it were to be erased. As a painter, she seems content that no attempt at explanation is required. Her stated aim is that the visitor to the centre may be diverted for a moment from their thoughts, engaged by the painting, to look and look again.

A fundamental question for all of these artists is how they would feel if their work were to be overpainted or treated in an inconsiderate manner. Sinta Tantra noted that in Balinese culture, art is embedded in the everyday rather than set apart. Many weeks may be spent creating epic structures for festivals that are burnt or broken up and distributed. The tradition has deeper spiritual significance in relation to reincarnation. She finds it liberating, therefore, to give her work to an audience for as long as it has a meaningful purpose.

MORAG MYERSCOUGH: THE AUDIENCE

A common factor that unites the majority of the selected artists is that they are aware that their art is not being made primarily for themselves. Despite a view that they might earn a better living as gallery artists, one is left with a clear impression that they feel more contented having found this way of working, finding satisfaction from making art that has a social purpose. What would be regarded as 'Public Art' – commissioned for an external space and for a wholly public audience – is not the focus here, although some of the artists have also undertaken commissioned public projects.

Morag Myerscough (b. 1963) is based in London and frequently works in open-air environments for and with communities. She is commissioned as an artist and there is an expectation of leadership; and the brief, purpose and occasionally the implementation may be a collective endeavour. This book is focused on permanently embedded art within architecture, and three projects exemplify her approach to such situations: Sheffield Children's Hospital, 2017 (with Avanti Architects and commissioner Cat Powell from Artfelt); University Hospital at Linköping, Sweden, 2017–18 (with White Architects, curator/art consultant Ann Magnusson); and 1 Finsbury Avenue, London, 2019 (renovated by architects AHMM). In each case, the specific target audience – as well as the physical space in which the piece is situated – became part of the way in which she conceived the work.

The most unusual project is at Sheffield. Almost invariably, spatial art in architecture is located in circulation spaces, in foyers, or occasionally in a room of particular significance. This project challenges this paradigm, but in doing so, several additional barriers had to be negotiated for the project to be successfully implemented. The new hospital wing provides bedroom accommodation for children, sometimes in long-stay situations, and therefore the family of the patients may also be visiting the room for several months. The aim was to use the artwork to shift the perception of the space, to de-institutionalise the rooms and make them feel more homely and less sterile in appearance, while remaining clinically and practically functional. Myerscough introduced artwork on wall surfaces, the soffits of fold-down beds, doors and cupboards (fig.6.6). Initial responses from the hospital staff were sceptical and resistant, and the artist was required to make small models to demonstrate the proposal. These were very useful devices to win over the users. Part of this process also influenced the colour palette, with a soft blue/green version made for some rooms to appeal to children who have conditions like autism and may have an intolerance to bright patterns. While this extended development process, interacting with future building users, is expected as part of the work of architects or interior designers, it is more unusual for an artist – and highly unlikely for a gallery artist. In this case, the work challenged so many

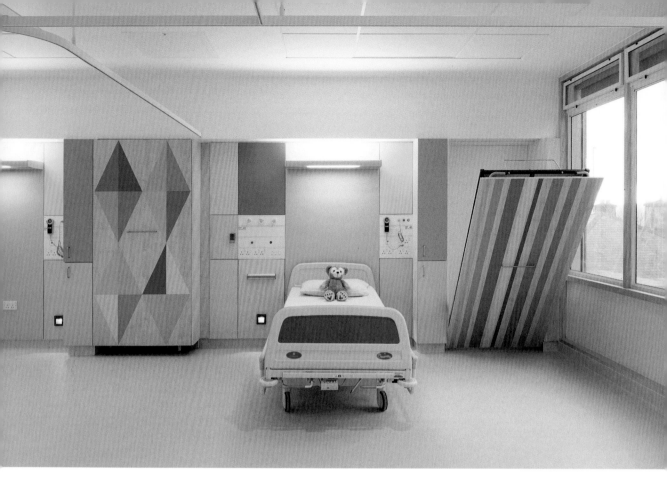

6.6　Morag Myerscough, laminate board, Sheffield Children's Hospital (Avanti Architects and Artfelt), 2017

preconceptions that the commissioner, Cat Powell – who is dedicated to this children's hospital – had a crucial role in managing and giving confidence to the stakeholders.

Further logistical challenges related to the choice of materials, such as working with a laminate manufacturer to develop the finish. In most of her artwork, Myerscough paints directly onto surfaces using acrylic paint. She avoids techniques like applied digital vinyl, which gives a reflective surface and an apparent superficiality. In this project, the laminate provides a flat, dense colour but meets stringent performance specifications. In many respects, the Sheffield project may be thought of as interior design as much as it is spatial art. The project was highly collaborative, with Mary Reid, Avanti Architects' interior designer, working closely with Myerscough. The skill of the artist has often

been to question the norm, to act as an agent for change, to push and challenge accepted thinking. Artwork in hospitals, particularly for children, can often be childish both in its expression and in the colours chosen. The commissioner was keen to use a 'professional' artist, and Myerscough was selected in the full knowledge that her work could be controversial. The artwork radically shifts the experience of the space, and there are tangible effects that go beyond the spatial experience. The colour and artwork appear to have made significant improvements to recovery times. None of this is surprising as the use of colour within hospital environments has long been known to have such effects and is a significant research topic.[6] Many UK hospital trusts have a parallel charitable organisation to raise funds to enhance the experience of hospital users. This includes commissioning artwork as well as staging activities and events. Sensitivity and courage are required on the part of the art commissioner, who may also advocate for professional work. The nature, extent and materiality of Myerscough's intervention was negotiated through conversations directly with her audience, but critically, without compromising the integrity and ambition of the artwork.

Finding a balance between the space and the artwork in terms of the experience of the architecture requires trust, particularly on the part of the client. At 1 Finsbury Avenue, Broadgate, Paul Monaghan of architects AHMM suggested Myerscough be invited to make a permanent installation in a very large, double-height space. The building, which is Grade II listed, was originally designed by Peter Foggo of Arup Associates in the 1980s in restrained black steel and glass. The renovation, completed in 2019, marks a significant shift from a hermetic corporate world to one that allows greater public permeability. Myerscough's *Atoll* project could not make more of a contrast in this environment and may be thought to dominate entirely, pushing the architecture into the background. The focal point is a cafe designed as a free-standing object, occupying the space both physically and optically. Intensely bright ceramic tiles form a robust base and introduce an abstracted narrative derived from the historical street patterns. The structure is topped by steel frames (suggesting the terraced houses that were demolished to make way for the commercial developments) and finally with an array of discs – conceived of as 'suns'. Myerscough recalls that the commission nearly floundered over this element, but the client was persuaded to make a leap of faith and it was completed without compromise. The suns may be read as symbolic, but they have the effect of extending the eye upwards into the black void of space (fig.6.7). From the upper mezzanine, the work is seen very differently, and without the tall spires might have felt too anchored to the floor. The size and positioning of the artwork is fundamental, and Myerscough was able to use the experience of her external works to find an appropriate scale. She enjoys exploiting height in order to shift the viewpoint upwards from the normal horizontal plane. Myerscough is very aware that her use

of colour may be controversial and that some architects asked to work with her may take a sharp intake of breath, aware that the architecture may struggle to compete. Perhaps it is understandable, therefore, that her work is often sited in spaces that are otherwise neutral, forming a backdrop that allows the colour insertions to become the focus of attention, intertwined with the memory of the place (fig.6.8).

A second hospital project, in Sweden, is perhaps more conventional: a large-scale work sited in a circulation space. The point at which an artist becomes involved in a collaborative project is significant. In this project, Myerscough was invited to collaborate at an early stage, before any building work had commenced.[7] Few artists relish working on site at the same time as multiple contractors and note that there is an optimum period towards completion and before the handover. It is also unusual to be working solely with drawings and over an extended period that may strain the economics of the commission. The artwork, over 200 metres in length, is sited in the main public 'spine' corridor (fig.6.9). Given the unexpectedly long gestation period, Myerscough made use of the time to generate her conceptual idea for the piece. It draws on a year-long project, *Colour Mood Tweets*, that catalogues an instinctive reaction to her personal mood each day. The international audience for the 'Tweets' knew nothing of the project, nothing was explained, and it appeared as a random but rhythmical pulse of the artist's feelings translated and indexed to colour. Although highly personal, the work anticipates its audience and embeds that knowledge as part of its production. Myerscough is not suggesting that there is a universal link between a singular hue and emotion, as is frequently and simplistically portrayed, but rather that one individual's emotional state might demonstrate that fluctuations in mood are ubiquitous and routine, and that in a hospital environment human emotional experience can change in an instant. For Myerscough, it is vital that all her work has meaning, that there is an intellectual depth that is layered within the work. Although conscious that she has become known for colour and pattern, the meaning embedded throughout her works goes beyond surface decoration.

6.7 and 6.8   Morag Myerscough, *Atoll*, 2019 (with architects AHMM), ceramic tile, acrylic paint, steel, 1 Finsbury Avenue, London

6.9   Morag Myerscough, *Colour Mood Tweets*, 2019, acrylic paint on plywood, University Hospital, Linköping, Sweden

While the architects discussed in Chapter 3 used a painterly or artistic approach – not necessarily knowing in advance how the work would develop – Myerscough's work in hospital contexts tends to be mapped out to scale, adjusted and developed through a 'designerly' method. The choice of colours in her work has become recognisable as a palette, although the actual colours are not consistent between projects. There is a clarity to many of the hues that the artist uses – they are generally saturated, with a hint of white that edges away from a pure hue. She refers to visiting an exhibition, *Hockney Paints the Stage* at the Hayward Gallery (1983), as a pivotal moment; Hockney being a vivid example of an artist who has the confidence to use colour in his work. Similarly, the Op-Art of the 1960s, including Bridget Riley's work, continues to be influential.

Myerscough's artwork for Linköping appears flat. The forms are geometric and have a graphic quality clearly applied as two-dimensional shapes. In terms of its spatial effect, the immediacy of the saturated colour is likely to precede any reading of form. In some of her temporary and external projects, she uses text extruded in form with a black shadow to give an illusion of depth, but also to give emphasis and legibility to the message, which sets the letters apart from the saturated colour of the background. As at Broadgate, some of the public art installations are also fixed to a skeletal structure and so have an actual architectural presence of volume. In the long wall painting at Linköping, the acute angle of view of the surface is significant, as is the movement of the viewer. The spatial experience of the painting appears to be generated by the composition and juxtaposition of colour and the rhythm of various scales of the triangular forms, which cause the eye to dart across the surface, making different formal constructions. The use of exposed plywood within the piece acts as a counterpoint to the density of the acrylic paint. It is not a singular experience, however, as there is no 'one way' of reading the pattern.

A similar effect is apparent in the work of the Belgian artist Georges Meurant who employs overlapping rectangular forms in much of his work. His largest permanent installation is in the Europa Building in Brussels where councillors convene in a visually complex space, sandwiched between a polychromatic ceiling and radial carpet that is intended to symbolise the diversity of the peoples of the European Union.[8] The spatial effect of the colour and pattern in his work is clearer in his easel paintings. Rectangular forms of different scales are painted in vibrant hues. As the eye scans across a painting, it oscillates between the scales connecting smaller rectangles together, generating an illusion of larger rectangles. In Gestalt theory, colour is instrumental to our cognitive search for complete forms. Presented with multiple readings, the eye will hop from one shape to another. Jean Guirand, in an essay on Meurant's work, argues that the result is a pictorial space that is 'destined to wander'.[9] Each time the eye seeks to complete a formal reading, the interaction of the form and colour, field and ground re-configures, making for an unstable spatial experience. In Myerscough's wall painting, the active spatial experience is similarly multivalent and somewhat unpredictable. The viewer will be engaged in the work at some cognitive level through colour and form as they pass through an otherwise mundane corridor. Myerscough and the curator/art consultant Ann Magnusson were acutely aware, however, that the piece might be considered as visually confusing, particularly to people who were already stressed by being in hospital, or those with visual or neurological sensitivities. The proposed artwork triggered a series of consultations, as at Sheffield. The artwork challenged widely held beliefs that hospitals should use subdued blues and greens, and that pattern is to be avoided. Much of the nervousness was due to assumptions and to a dogmatic approach to the application of guidelines misinterpreted as facts. Once experts were directly consulted, however, they supported the installation. Ann Magnusson notes that there is a pedagogical role in her work – to help the users feel confident to take a risk. The artist also needs to be skilful in this respect and Magnusson was conscious that it is hard for people to believe in something abstract. In this case, however, the artwork has an inherent meaning beyond a purely decorative design, and she reports that since the work has been installed the reaction has been extremely supportive. The wall painting has become an aid to wayfinding, providing a memorable landmark and an uplifting injection of colour in an otherwise pristine, white environment.

TOBY PATERSON: IN RESPONSE TO CONTEXT

The German artist Blinky Palermo had a way of engaging with the viewer and the site through the most economical of means. A simple white line on an ochre background in an installation in Munich skirted around the edges of a wall, up and over a doorframe, with a corresponding ochre band on an adjacent white wall. His wall paintings were intended to draw attention to the architecture and to heighten the experience of moving through a space. Frequently they were sited in interstitial spaces, with many intended to be temporary. One celebrated example is a simple band of four colours, *Blue/Yellow/White/Red*, at cornice level around the staircase at the Edinburgh College of Art, painted in August 1970 as part of Richard Demarco's avant-garde show, *Strategy: Get Arts.* Despite pleas at the time to allow it to remain, it was overpainted, but then re-instated in 2005. However, it is barely noticed as it is seen in the peripheral vision, high up, shifting as the orientation of the viewer changes. That is, of course, partly the point of the work. A paradox of such unobtrusiveness is that the work can be misread as simplistic, implacable and lacking in an emotional engagement. It does not scream for attention – it is there to be discovered, or not (fig.6.10).

The contemporary Scottish artist Toby Paterson (b. 1974) took a similar position in making a series of artworks, *Thresholds*, commissioned for each of the Maggie's Cancer Care Centres in Scotland (fig.6.11). The pieces are typical of his work. Three-dimensional, modest in scale (varying between 15–30 cm [5 ⅞–11 ¹³⁄₁₆ in]), subtly painted in soft tones of acrylic paint on machined, constructed

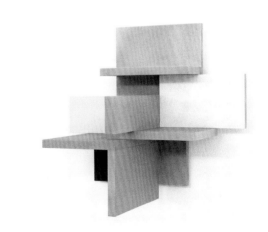

TOP

6.10   Blinky Palermo, *Blue/Yellow/White/Red*, 1970, reconstructed artwork at Edinburgh College of Art, 2005

BOTTOM

6.11   Toby Paterson, *Crooked Path*, 2015, acrylic on aluminium, 27 × 30.5 × 21 cm (10 ⅝ × 12 × 8 ¼ in)

aluminium, they are highly site-specific, made after extended periods of observation and working in collaboration with the architects and clients. Each piece has a criticality in its location that is intended to make an emotional engagement with the users and atmosphere of each site, revealing itself gradually with greater familiarity. His work carefully considers the potential mindset of the users, likely to be subject to radical swings in emotion in these places of sanctuary. The artwork responds through a spatial re-reading of the spaces inside and outside the building and by incorporating memories of colour, some of which are drawn from the immediate environment.

Paterson is first and foremost a painter, but has become known for working in relief. Like all the artists selected, colour is integral to his practice. He cannot always explain why certain colours are chosen, nor does he feel the need to have a specific reason. No colours are specifically taboo or overlooked, although some are repeated. He enjoys the idea of combining colours that may be dull or largely disliked, such as a muddy khaki green, enlivened by its proximity to orange and pale blue. There are noticeably less saturated hues, particularly in the works encountered on the edges of a space, but he does not shy away from moments of intensity or large areas of solid black. In a collaborative project with Collective Architects for the Paisley Museum, he became an ally in the development of a bold colour strategy and supergraphics. Understanding that the first encounter for the public would be in a transition space with no reception desk, where no one would linger, the response was to envelop the entrance volume in an immersive, intense yellow that glows into the street at night.

Paterson feels comfortable engaging with the practical aspects of his commissions, and this can also mean being invited to work within buildings that are utilitarian and where there is little that is resonant in the architecture. If an ultimate goal is to make artwork that is inseparable from its architectural context, his aim shifts in a prosaic building to enhance and intensify the sense of place in an otherwise mute environment. An example is his work within the Minerva Primary Academy in Bristol, *A Shift in Perspective* (2017). It is significant that the artist and commissions

manager identified a total of nine opportunities within the school for different, site-specific forms of artwork. The project is a form of art by stealth, wrestling with a low budget to tweak mundane architectural elements – for example, a canopy with stripes of pale blue and red that cast light on the surfaces below, a perforated privacy screen that invites touch, the use of signage and two large wall paintings that bookend the plan in the stairwells. The two paintings, although set physically apart, are counterpoints. In one, red, pale blue and cream forms float on a black background. In the other, the same palette is transposed to black, red and cream on pale blue (fig.6.12). The paintings help with orientation but are also bound to leave an impression on the staff and students. Already, the artwork has become synonymous with the school. Without it, the experience and memories of this building would be substantially diminished.

Any artist who makes an installation directly on the wall or ceiling surfaces is aware that their work is vulnerable, not only through the potential demise or change of use of the container, but also to poor maintenance or the shifting nature of public understanding of the significance of the work. Some works may be well cared for, such as Victor Pasmore's mural, *Metamorphosis*, in the Renold Building in Manchester (architects Cruickshank & Seward, 1962). Paterson quips that the Pasmore painting is so well loved that it has developed a thick tidemark as the university painters carefully re-paint around its edges. By contrast, Pasmore's large *Apollo Pavilion* sculpture in Peterlee New Town (1969) suffered decades of vandalism and neglect until it was finally restored in 2009.[10] At the Glasgow Caledonian University campus, Toby Paterson was commissioned in 2005 to make three monumental paintings called *Potential Forms* in the Saltire Centre. Two paintings with a white background were made on the flank wall panels, which are set at an angle to the space; the third – with a floating turquoise oval and red, white, and ochre ribbons on a black base – anchors the rear wall surface. Rather than lurking quietly in corners awaiting discovery, as in the Maggie's Centre series, these works occupy and define the character of the space (fig.6.13). The building was subsequently extended and re-configured by Page\Park Architects in 2015, forcing a large

RIGHT

6.12 Toby Paterson, *A Shift in Perspective*, 2017, eggshell on plaster, installation view at Minerva Primary Academy, Bristol, 2018

RIGHT

6.12 Toby Paterson, *A Shift in Perspective*, 2017, eggshell on plaster, installation view at Minerva Primary Academy, Bristol, 2018

BELOW

6.13 Toby Paterson, *Potential Forms*, 2005, acrylic and eggshell on wall, triptych dimensions variable, installation view at Glasgow Caledonian University

6.14   Toby Paterson, *Cluster Relief (River)*, 2016, acrylic on aluminium, 145 × 1235 × 12.5 cm
(57 ¹⁄₁₆ × 486 ¼ × 4 ¹⁵⁄₁₆ in), installation view at Glasgow Caledonian University

opening to be constructed directly through the wall painting. Paterson is sanguine about its fate, even to the extent that he feels the opening has added a pleasing tension. The work itself is now read differently, and the hole now frames a view to one of a new series of artworks that he has made for the extension.

The artist has created a series of relief works for various locations, which aim to engage the viewer and add multiple readings to the space in which they are sited.[11] *Cluster Relief (River)* (2016) for Glasgow Caledonian University – an array of tilted rectilinear panels – is wall-mounted along a linear route from the entrance and visible from the outside (fig.6.14). The works change in appearance in perspective view with the movement of the viewer in parallax. Scattered, clear red panels are much more apparent in one direction, angled in plan towards the doorway. Pale blue panels in two tones vie with red-brown planes in the other direction. The work is sited in strong daylight, adding shadow play to the dynamic shifts of colour and form.

A further work – a mobile – is suspended within a void of a circular stair and is therefore experienced from multiple viewpoints. Paterson is clearly not afraid to work on a large scale; for example, his *Poised Array* (2007), a 'fizzy cluster of colours' set adjacent to the sombre facade of David Chipperfield Architects' BBC Scotland building on the banks of the River Clyde in Glasgow; and a collaboration with Cullinan Studio/McGurk Architects at the Bunhill 2 Energy Station in London (2020). There is, nevertheless, a modesty in his conception. Reflecting on his embedded works, Paterson explains: 'I hope they work in an ambient way. They are placed so that you experience them as you move through the buildings and can be ignored as much as noticed, but subconsciously they will register.'[12]

Significantly, in terms of collaborative work, Paterson tunes into post-war architecture in his paintings and reliefs, with some works depicting architectural space in a representational manner. In terms of pictorial space, Paterson approaches each piece in relation to its location, each having 'the pictorial space it deserves'.[13] His aim is to amplify the experience by reflecting the spatial qualities of the space back to the viewer. The result is a heightened sensibility to both art and architecture, through subtle shifts in perception and a tuning of the subconscious experience using colour and form.

MARK TITCHNER: A TONE OF VOICE

The US artist Barbara Kruger's strident red, black and white images sear into the eye and mind. Although most of her works were conceived to be viewed in gallery settings, the choice of colour and typeface shout loudly, the power of the spoken word translated to visual typographic artwork. Direct text messages have a complex psychological effect on the viewer, particularly if their meaning is ambiguous, or where the setting is incongruous. If the work also includes colour, there will be a

hierarchy in the way the work connects with the audience, with text and colour competing for attention. Jenny Holzer (b. 1950), the contemporary US artist, makes use of external billboards – sometimes on the sides of mobile trucks – to address her audience with powerful, carefully constructed words that appear as politically driven slogans. A profoundly moving black and white photograph of Felix Gonzalez-Torres' (1957–96) unmade bed, *Untitled* (1991), taken immediately after the death of his partner from AIDS, was posted at 24 street locations (to mark the date of his death). This imprint of intimacy, deliberately out of context, speaks softly and intensely without words. External billboards, conventionally associated with advertising, attract attention because of their scale and location, and because we are accustomed to receiving messages in this manner.

London-based artist Mark Titchner (b. 1973) – who often works with typography and with pattern and colour – cites these artists as influential in his own work. He conceives of each artwork as having a particular 'tone of voice'. Not only is there a message, but the means of communicating it is modulated through its artistic expression. The context for each work is key to finding the right tone. Like the US artists, he started his career by using external found surfaces, such as bus stops and billboards. His works are infused with ambiguity and doubt, and the audience may be confused as to the origin of the message. During the pandemic of 2020, one of his artworks that had originally been made in 2012 was reworked with a different, louder colour palette and bold black text to be printed in poster form. This appears as an unambiguous message – *Please Believe These Days Will Pass* – that seemed to chime with the emotional needs of humanity. The work appeared across multiple billboards in the UK and Europe, distributed by a third party. The artwork found a tone of voice that resonated with its audience. What was deliberately ambiguous, at least before social media stepped in to clarify, was the source of the work. People thought it was a government message or an invocation from a pseudo-religious organisation (fig.6.15).[14]

In an external permanent work for Camden Council, London, *Not For Self But For All* (2014), Titchner wrapped the topmost corner of the building with an LED-illuminated artwork. It is conceived almost as a digital stained-glass window. He considers that 'there is a degree of hubris in the commissioning of the piece'. The colour here can be much brighter as it is generated by light, and the tones are more saturated than in painted or printed artworks, so that it acts as a beacon and landmark that references the large, illuminated advertising signs and texts that shout out at passers-by. The intended 'volume', as well as the tone of voice of the piece, is a combination of colour – moderated by the material choice – but also through a balancing of typeface, of the pattern behind and of the interaction between the colours (fig.6.16).

Titchner has made a number of installations in psychiatric wards commissioned by the charity Hospital Rooms. Finding a tone for these works requires a level of sensitivity to the users

and to the staff, but it is common to find that such institutions are overcautious in the use of colour, resulting in bland and under-stimulating environments. His approach is highly collaborative, fully understanding the need to engage the users – sometimes directly – in the making of the work. In some situations, for example, colour is kept soft, with minimal differentiation between the figure of the type and the ground of the pattern. The artwork whispers to the viewer. In others, where the environment may be monotonous or dull, a more vibrant palette may be chosen. A common expectation in mental health environments is that there is a need for calm, but people may long for vibrant colour to take them out of the visually drab surroundings. Unusually, he may offer the users a choice of colour options, involving the staff who will live with the piece every day. Most critically

6.15   Mark Titchner, *Please Believe These Days Will Pass*, 2020, billboard poster (a collaboration between Mark Titchner and JACK ARTS)

6.16 Mark Titchner, *Not For Self But For All*, 2014, digital print on vinyl, LED lightbox, King's Cross, London

6.17 Mark Titchner, *Together We Can Do So Much*, 2019, veneered Valchromat and acrylic paint, Zayed Centre for Research into Rare Diseases in Children, Great Ormond Street Hospital, London

for Titchner, he prefers to make the artwork in situ, painting directly on the wall, so that the users see his work, with its imperfections, pencil and brush marks on the surface. They are not only involved in the discussion, but witness the art being made by hand. There is an acknowledged investment in the time spent by the artist in the ward, through which he personally feels a sense of achievement. By contrast his billboards are intended to feel inhuman – printed by machine – a generic blankness in terms of execution, suited to the setting of the advertising hoarding. Titchner negotiates between work that is highly site-specific, where he will often seek meaning in the social and cultural history of the place, and others that are non-specific, generic and aimed at unknown audiences. In each case the use of colour will be modified in response.

At the Zayed Centre for Research into Rare Diseases in Children (2019), a new facility designed by architects Stanton Williams as part of Great Ormond Street Hospital, the colours chosen for a permanent artwork are a subtle palette of browns, ochres and pale blue. There are three different audiences for this piece, set by the section of the building and available lines of sight. The primary audience is the researchers themselves who work in a lower-ground-floor laboratory within a double-height volume. Pedestrians can look directly down into the space from the street, and across to the artwork. Finally, other building users look across to the artwork from a bridge over the laboratory below as they enter the building. The siting for the work was identified by the architects and client, and Titchner's work responds to this multi-level setting. The pale blue evokes the upward gaze of the scientists to the sky, while the text, *Together We Can Do So Much*, reaches beyond a singular audience. Here, the setting meant that the colour tone would not distract. The artwork enhances the building by the introduction of colour within the predominately clinical environment, but is also intended to enhance the everyday experience of all the users through the embedded message (fig.6.17).

Just as Titchner will tweak the colours used to find a suitable 'tone of voice', he will also try to flatten the perceptual space of the work to avoid a visual hierarchy, so will deliberately boost the saturation of the background when the text is bolder to 'resist the primacy of the text'. Beyond any sense of spatial depth within the artwork, therefore, there is perhaps a more significant spatial effect that could be articulated as the cognitive space in the minds of the viewer. One can argue that all artworks will act in this way to some extent, but words, particularly ones that are ambiguous or unclear in their meaning, may be glimpsed, received and internalised in the mind of the viewer, only to re-emerge in their thoughts at a later moment. Although the colour may act immediately to grab attention, the words will be processed in a different way psychologically. Viewers will search to make sense of what they have seen – or in this case, what they have read. For example, at London Bridge Station, Titchner was commissioned to make an artwork, titled *Me. Here. Now.* (2018), for a Victorian brick-vaulted circulation route. He was aware that commuters tend to have their minds elsewhere and may be in a sort of mental reverie, or detached by the use of headphones, distracted by thoughts of their journey, thus, rarely actively engaged in the environment. The tunnel site makes this mindset acute, with very large numbers of people walking past, barely conscious of the context. Titchner particularly enjoys settings where people are on the move and in a state of distraction, going or coming from somewhere, where the site of the artwork is not a destination in itself. Here, in a complex collaborative project where multiple disciplines and stakeholders were involved, Titchner proposed three massive, mirrored domes that he notes were 'unequivocal in their scale'. The faceted surfaces appear almost slippery as the reflections and colours constantly change with the passage of the people beneath (fig.6.18). The intention is to disengage people momentarily from their distracted isolation and to re-engage them within their physical and social context. The reflection of the viewer is distorted by the form of the dome to produce unexpected reflections of a single viewer

6.18   Mark Titchner, *Me. Here. Now.*, 2018, digital print on mirrored steel, London Bridge Station

paused for an instant among the multiple moving figures of others. The words that are printed onto the surfaces evoke travel and journeys in a direct way, but also invite people to pause and reflect on their journeys in a more philosophical, or even spiritual, way. There is a further level of spatial deception as the giant domes may appear to be transparent chandeliers, looking through to the brickwork. These extraordinarily heavy structures can appear weightless through the perceptual manipulation. In common with other artists, the appeal of making a site-specific piece is to tune into the context and amplify the existing architecture. The domes may be almost invisible, may go unnoticed, but have the potential to stimulate the viewer, if only fleetingly.

A sense of spatial depth is also manifested through Titchner's very varied material practices, such as mass-produced digital prints or hand paintings using acrylic or commercial emulsion, sometimes sealed for ease of maintenance. In his printed billboard and gallery works that are usually composed digitally, there is often a layering with superimposed images, sometimes with varied levels of transparency to introduce interference between the layers. At the Zayed Centre he collaborated with a fabricator in the making of the work using the Portuguese product 'Valchromat', which is an exceptionally stable and robust, wood-fibre board that allows for a chlorine clean when required. The material was laminated with a wood veneer and then hand painted with 'Liquitex' acrylic paint. The work combines digital production with CNC-routered channels, giving a literal depth in the thickness of the material. At One St Peter's Square, a commercial building in Manchester designed by Glen Howells Architects, Titchner was commissioned to make two site-specific works – *Dream after Dream after Dream* and *Live the Life That You Imagine* (2015). In the first work, letters appear to dissolve in the reflections and refractions of mirrored acrylic, while the second work is a lightbox that acts as a beacon at the end of a dark hallway. Throughout Titchner's work, the choice of material, colour and words introduces multiple layers of meaning that are balanced both visually and in the way in which the artwork might be seen to address the cognitive space of the viewer.

TESS JARAY: AT INTERVALS

For nearly 40 years, London commuters have raced or ambled across the eastern concourse at Victoria Station, mostly oblivious that they are walking on an artwork. Art is not normally expected to be located underfoot or in such an everyday place. The station concourse is far from a grand terminal space and is the architectural result of an awkward clash between two rival train companies, terminating in an irregular crescent form.[15] The terrazzo floor by Tess Jaray, completed in 1985, is one of several public paving commissions. Her largest project, for Centenary Square in Birmingham (1991), was decommissioned in 2019 and the majority of the work removed, after suffering from heavy traffic and poor maintenance of the concrete block paviours. The Victoria Station concourse – in a deep plum and terracotta-red terrazzo, set within a conventional white flooring – has endured, perhaps because of its modesty and the way it seems to sit unassumingly amongst the visual chaos (fig.6.19). The colour relates directly to the surrounding facades of Portland stone, red brick and granite base, while the main axial orientation follows the structural line of the main beams and rooflight of Sir John Fowler's original station structure (1862) overhead. The dark colour of the paving anchors the floor and feels calming compared to the white surround, and the artwork invites a moment of pause to coincide with the main digital signboard. Even such a surreptitiously placed artwork will influence the architectural space and the experience of the user.

At the time of its execution, Jaray had been making paintings in which geometric trapezoidal forms distort and diminish in scale across the canvas, for example, *Kima* (1981; 213 × 213 cm) and *Minaret (Green)* (1984; 164 × 146 cm). An earlier commission for the British Pavilion at the Canadian Expo '67 in Montreal, designed by Basil Spence, had led Jaray to a shift in scale from easel to mural. The 450m² station concourse allowed a further shift in scale. Although her *Minaret* series seems to directly influence the geometry of the Victoria Station concourse, Richard Cork stresses that the works are representative of her more general explorations at that time and were never intended to be studies for the flooring.[16]

One of the most distinctive features of her work is her use of colour and pattern. Born in Vienna in 1937, before settling with her parents as exiles in England in 1938, she trained at St

Martin's School of Art and the Slade School of Art in London in the late 1950s. Her understanding of colour has developed over a lifetime of painting and printmaking. In an essay, 'Red: The Diary of a Painting', in her insightful book *Painting: Mysteries and Confessions*, she writes of the tantalising search for a specific hue and her disappointment when a red appears as too pure or too flat and the distorting spatial effect of a saturated hue. Her paintings may emerge from the silent space in the middle of the night for no specific reason, and, once applied, the colours make demands relative to each other and on the viewer: 'how curious that a painting that started with silence should be getting so noisy'.[17] She has used tones of vivid turquoise and shocking pink, but much of her work since the mid-1960s has a softer and more subtle range of hue and tone. For example, in artworks she employs a pale pinkish-purple with dark teal green, olive greens on mid-green, tawny pink, soft ochre and warm grey to near black-green and very dark aubergine. Colour is constantly used spatially to create dynamic shifts in the apparent depth of the pictorial space, but also as a fundamental definition of rhythm, pattern, boundaries and edges. Her canvas paintings – for example, *Rialto* (1966) – have an architectural and spatial quality, with distinctive multiple parallel lines that have trouble connecting sweetly together and resemble the way in which fluted stone vaulting must negotiate its complex three-dimensional form. The use of multiple parallel lines appears in the terrazzo pattern for Victoria Station. The gap between each plum-coloured diamond is expressed as a white line that allows the eye to read each diminishing section. It would have been easier to make a conventional pattern of equal forms; indeed one might anticipate that this would have been the response if the floor had been designed by an architect. Instead, the artwork is a very subtle play of rhythm and quasi-perspective that plays with the moving pedestrian and the low angle of view. The floor may be conceived in plan, but Jaray's work understands how it will be experienced on foot. There is a tension between the regularity and symmetry of the form in one axis and the gradual reduction in the size of each area, but the large scale of the pieces – seen from the viewpoint of the pedestrian – makes it appear

6.19   Tess Jaray, *Victoria Station Concourse*, 1985, terrazzo, London

that the distortion is caused by anamorphic movement, or rather that it becomes spatially ambiguous. Jaray always seeks a tension in her work – 'between absence and presence and the intervals between' – as though, if fully resolved by symmetry, the geometry would lose its dynamism.[18] Jaray's work is explicitly spatial. Her paintings may initially appear two-dimensional, but the pictorial depth generated in the work through colour and composition appears as one engages with the work. A fine pattern will be aligned in perfect rows at the lower edge, only to disintegrate in micro-rhythms, vertically. In each case, the geometry emanates from rhythms and minute shifts in the interval between one shape and the next, to create an expanding rhythm that may also give an illusion of three-dimensional

6.20 and 6.21   Tess Jaray, St Mary's in the Lacemarket, patterned stone floor, Cove Red and Ancaster Weatherbed Limestone, Nottingham, 2012

form. To Jaray, the space created in an artwork will contribute to the three-dimensional space within which it is viewed. Viewers may momentarily let themselves be drawn into the depth of the painting, and for a commission that one walks on as a surface, the spatial experience is even more complex. To work at the scale of architectural paving, Jaray studied the human gait, the rhythm and pacing of a stride, and what is comfortable and pleasurable to walk over. This serial interest in an expression of a spatial interval is explicit in her prints and paintings but has also informed her permanent commissions within architectural settings. At St Mary's in the Lacemarket, Nottingham (2012), a major commission for a patterned stone floor uses stripes of two colours of stone, a soft terracotta sandstone from Ayrshire and beige-grey Weatherbed Jurassic limestone from Ancaster in Lincolnshire (figs 6.20 and 6.21). Jaray's passion for pattern in architectural settings stems from an early period in Italy where the beauty of polychromatic marble floors had a profound influence. Reflecting on the Nottingham work, Jaray feels the contrast between the stones might have been more acute to emphasise the pattern. The softness of the tones does not call for attention as do the green and white marbles of Brunelleschi; rather it appears as though it has been there since the church itself, which was completed around 1470. The artwork is so embedded in the experience of the place as to largely go unnoticed.[19]

The relationship to the edge is also carefully considered. In her early paintings – for example, *Early Piazza* (1964) – and in her mural for Expo '67, the form confronts the edge of the canvas and is sometimes abruptly terminated, implying a continuation independent of the frame of view. In others, the pattern sits well within the edges, surrounded by a field of colour. In making the floors, the boundaries of the artwork must adjust to accommodate columns, inflections and irregularities. Her elegant piazza at the British

Embassy in Moscow, with architects ABK (2000), occupies the space and leads the visitor subtly to the entrance. The layout of the work suggests three distinct territories, generated by the perimeter of the building and as a symbolic bridge between the countries – a deep boundary at the gate, a threshold band of single colour, then the main central pattern in granite setts. A similar, more modest intervention was commissioned and gifted by Lord Palumbo for the terrace of the Arts Council of Great Britain, 1992. In this case, a green Kirkstone slate is contrasted with a near-white Bianco Lorca from Spain. Both works have a timeless quality intended to respond to the dignity of the buildings and inspired by Jaray's fascination with Italian floors and Islamic patterns that appear to mediate between containment and expansion.

Jaray is aware that her paintings sometimes gestate for years in her subconscious before something is triggered. An example is the *Aleppo*

series, one iteration of which is installed in the foyer space at the Tapestry Building in King's Cross, London, part of a large programme of art for the major redevelopment of the city quarter (fig.6.22). Here the tension of the boundary between the softly coloured panels is palpable, expressed as a violent jagged line, akin to Barnett Newman's 'zipped' boundaries. The abstract painting refers to her visit to the Syrian city before the destruction of the war. The striped patterns of mosques and lintels and zigzag lines were lodged in her memory, only to emerge much later in her work. Jaray's own paintings and the rhythmical pulse of geometry, colour and depth in the architectural installations may have a similar effect on the viewer. Where sited within architecture, the work has a compelling sense of order that echoes the structure, space and movement of people.

JASON BRUGES: INFRA-RED SHADOWS

We have become accustomed to associating colour with material surface. Although affected by surface reflectance, all colour is now known to be generated by light. Artists assimilate colour phenomena and become tuned to observing environmental colour in an acutely sensitive manner. In traditional figurative or representational painting an artist would know to use a warm yellow paint to suggest a white house at sunset. Yet the viewer will instinctively perceive the scene with a white house, glowing in the ambient light, despite the evidence of the paint on the canvas. The material colour is used to replicate a complex physiological and psychological experience of colour constancy.[20] Similarly, Goethe's observations that purplish-blue shadows are perceived to be cast by golden light from a candle, or by daylight on snow, were then replicated by impressionist artists, using the simultaneous hue contrast to accentuate the atmospheric effect.[21]

The work of Jason Bruges Studio uses light and colour to heighten our experience of space. For the other artists in this chapter, the concept of pictorial space in the artwork tends to be associated with the interrelationship of colours

and form, of an illusion of a space and depth behind the surface. In the case of Bruges' artwork, the pictorial space can be conceived as a series of planes in three-dimensional space in front of the surface as well as behind it. For Bruges – like the artists James Turrell, Daniel Buren and Ann Veronica Janssens – colour is a volumetric, atmospheric experience. In an early installation, *Pixel Cloud* (2007), an atrium is filled with point light sources. Rather than planar pixels, Bruges likens the spatial effect to 'voxels' distributed throughout a three-dimensional volume.

The basic parameters of colour are most easily conceived of in terms of hue, tone and saturation, but this only partly explains the phenomenon as experienced. An alternative is to think of a surface, a light source and a medium through which the colour is perceived. As noted previously, a painter may use paler tones to evoke distance because this is our experience of colour seen through a volume of air. If the medium is mist, as in the work of Olafur Eliasson (fig.5.30), the colour appears all around us reflected and refracted by the water droplets. Although this is possible with a temporary installation, many of Bruges' artworks are intended to be permanently embedded in their architectural setting. In starting a project, his early conversations with the client or architect will tend to revolve around finding a catalyst for the environmental experience, which may be tuned up or down in terms of its subtlety. The presence of the artwork invariably activates the space; the colour appears to linger in the air and inflect the feeling of a spatial setting. For example, in the large entrance foyer of a London commercial building, the overwhelming feeling is of calmness. The artwork *Perlin Canopy* – a cloud of circular hoops of fluctuating light – evokes the dappled light through a bower of trees, as may have once covered the site. Pale blue and white appears like a cloud-filled sky (fig.6.23).

Bruges trained as an architect and worked with Foster and Associates before setting up his studio in 2002. His interest in environmental psychology dates to his education at Oxford Brookes University. There he was taught by Professor Byron Mikellides, who was one of the few people within an architecture school teaching colour from the perspective of colour psychology

LEFT

6.22   Tess Jaray, *Aleppo*, 2017, acrylic paint on MDF, 51.8 × 32 cm (20 ⅜ × 12 ⅝ in), King's Cross, London

6.23   Jason Bruges, *Perlin Canopy* (AHMM Architects), 2018, 80 individually addressable LED rings, The Bower, Old Street, London

and human experience. In terms of artistic influences, Jason Bruges points to the light artists Dan Flavin, David Batchelor and Jim Campbell. But his interest in engaging the audience also draws on performative work and video artists. The theatricality of his artworks refers to architects such as Mark Fisher and Jonathan Park, who conjured up atmospheric installations as dramatic

settings for Pink Floyd and U2 concerts. In the case of Bruges, his artwork is embedded in the everyday life of streets and buildings. It is intended to spark one's curiosity, to engage the viewer momentarily. It invites interpretation that may include a misunderstanding of the complex nature of the artwork, leading to a conclusion that is not necessarily factually correct.

Many of Bruges' artworks make use of the movement of the human body as the trigger for change in colour and patterns. The technology of the light source is central to this contemporary artist's work. He chooses the colour of light as a painter might choose paint. In his case, the choice might be to reach for a pure orange light-emitting diode (LED). The colour is precise, defined by the wavelength of light emitted. As in a painting, the selection of hue is used to denote meaning, to tap into associations. Orange light, for example, is often used in industrial coding to indicate movement. In an installation for Broadwick House, London (2007) by architects Rogers Stirk and Harbour + Partners, day-time movements of lifts are monitored, then used in the evening to program multiple orange lights that mimic the movement of the lifts when they have become stationary at the end of the working day. The contrast of the light against its background is as significant as the figure-ground in painting, and the light reflectance of adjacent materials is part of the composition of the scene. At Great Ormond Street Hospital, an interactive, figurative installation, *Nature Trail* (2012), also uses orange/yellow lights set behind a printed wallpaper surface to create woodland animals to distract children on their way to the operating theatre. Although the lights are simply programmed by motion 'gates' along the corridor, the illusion is that the animals move along with the child (fig.6.24). The surface colours are pale blues, greys and green – commonly used in hospital environments, but which by themselves can appear too sterile. The contrast of the animated orange lights lifts the feeling of the corridor space and can be enjoyed by users of all ages.

A second use of colour in Bruges' work is to trigger cultural meaning and associations. In Eugene, Oregon, a wall installation, *Game Show* (2011), uses a live action feed from a basketball court nearby to trigger change in the colour of a multi-faceted surface. The local team are known as The Ducks, and the colours used suggest the yellow and green feathers of mallards. In most cultures, colour names emerge from flora and fauna, triggered by associations with nature. The studio has made several sophisticated works that adopt a form of abstracted biomimicry. A large artwork, *Dichroic*

6.24   Jason Bruges, *Nature Trail*, 2012, dichroic lamps set behind printed wallpaper, Great Ormond Street Hospital

Blossom (2014), set in a building by Foster and Partners in Beijing, uses a wall of dichroic prisms to refract white light, producing magenta and spring-green light in varying patterns to suggest plum blossom on trees (fig.6.25). The work is site-specific, in its relationship to both the architectural space – which is predominately in brown and white subdued tones – and also to the social and cultural context of China. Further works play on bio-luminescent creatures that emit a blue-green light, or insects and birds that act as pollinators, which are attracted by the inflorescence of plants. There is a fascinating paradox between the ephemeral technology of the artistic production and its

6.25   Jason Bruges, *Dichroic Blossom*, 2014, periscope LED light engines, bespoke mirror optics, bespoke dichroic crystals, IP camera, control system, 142.5 × 100 × 3 cm (56 ⅛ × 39 ⅜ × 1 ³⁄₁₆ in), Beijing

grounding in enduring natural phenomena of colour, light, and nature. Human perception of colour is limited to the visible spectrum, while insects and other life forms can see ultraviolet and infrared light. In one artwork, *Shadow Wall* (2019), in an urban underpass, unseen infrared light is detected by embedded sensors that react to the 'shadows' of people moving in the dark space, triggering visible white light patterns. As with all embedded artwork, there is a vulnerability to work set permanently into architectural settings. There will be decay in all work, and at some point maintenance will be required. Bruges must also consider how the work will look when switched off, and how the technology and materials can best be recycled.

These artworks engage the audience in a very different sensory way than a painting or a physical sculpture. The use of colour and movement is essentially joyful, but they are as open to interpretation as any artwork and are intended to challenge and to offer the viewer a moment of enquiry, and to draw attention to the specific spatial setting.

The absolute lack of constraint in studio art may appeal to artists in comparison to the logistical complexity, vulnerability and incidental relationship with its audience of work made for an architectural setting. Paradoxically, however, these same restraints challenge artists to produce work that resonates with the place in which it is situated – to revel in a shift of scale, to work on a surface that may be walked on, glimpsed, or leant against. While these examples have focused on the dialogue between the individual artist and the architecture, Part III will consider collaborative practices that bring clients, commissioners, architects and artists together.

PART III

CONSTRUCTING THE INSEPARABLE

7 Collaborative Practices

Mark Pimlott has pinpointed a fundamental hurdle to the successful synthesis of art and architecture: 'for artists to project their work onto architecture as it is made, there must be architects willing to accommodate it', adding that 'unsurprisingly there are relatively few architects who embrace such collaborations and their potential for disruption'.[1] There are, however, notable instances where such interactions have proved productive, and in the examples that follow, the use of colour has been a significant catalyst for the emergence of varied, symbiotic practices.

The Italian architect Gio Ponti championed an interaction between art, design and architecture. As founding editor of *Domus* magazine, he was able to influence generations of architects and designers. His own development – from early works in ceramics and hesitant mural paintings at the Palazzo del Bo, University of Padua (completed in 1937) (fig.7.1), through his long career as an architect and designer – is well documented in a decade-by-decade account, *Gio Ponti*, edited by Ugo La Pietra.[2] Ponti's work is representative of the notion of a *Gesamtkunstwerk* (total work of art), driven by an holistic design concept, that traverses all scales, from cutlery and crockery to furniture and architecture, and where colour made an important contribution. His Villa Planchart in Caracas, Venezuela (1955) and hotels in Sorrento (1962) and Rome are exemplary projects of this oeuvre. The Villa Planchart has a wide, but carefully co-ordinated, colour palette in greys, yellows, greens, mustard

and white, set against polychromatic marble floors and ceilings with sculpted reliefs or bold stripes. The Sorrento hotel, set high above the Mediterranean coast, has a restricted colour range, predominately of white and blue, but with multiple patterns in the floor tiles, wall ceramics, textiles and furniture, and through a variety of textures, from shiny round blue pebbles set into the render, to a smooth ultramarine laminate against red-brown veneer (fig.7.2). Many of his prototype designs for tiles, pebbles and furniture were subsequently developed as manufactured products, and Ponti's wide-ranging output has continued to be influential in the work of, for example, the polymath Ettore Sottsass.[3] Neither sought a singular vision. One might classify their approach as a continuation of the early 20th-century Arts and Crafts movement and the pre-war Deutscher Werkbund, which pre-dated the Bauhaus and promoted close association across disciplines in arts education and production.[4] While the Arts and Crafts impulse was retrospectively nostalgic in outlook, the Bauhaus was experimental and formative, as were Ponti and Sottsass.

LEFT

7.1   Gio Ponti, Palazzo del Bo foyer, architecture and mural paintings by Ponti, University of Padua, 1937

ABOVE RIGHT

7.2   Gio Ponti, hotel, Sorrento, Italy, 1962 (renovated 2020)

Here, we are concerned more with the coming together of art and architecture through autonomous practices with graded scales of interaction, from the wholly independent artist commissioned to make a site-specific work in a completed project, to a fully intertwined co-authored project, or simply an enriched dialogue that fortifies each party in some way intellectually but may not have a defined output. There is a question that must be answered: what makes a collaboration successful?

ARCHITECT-LED COLLABORATIONS

One of the most celebrated examples of the integration of art and architecture is at the central campus of the University of Caracas (Ciudad Universitaria) in Venezuela, South America, which was underpinned by cultural exchange, sustained friendships and mutual respect between collaborators. Carlos Raúl Villanueva was born in London in 1900 of French and Venezuelan parents and trained at the École des Beaux-Arts in Paris, before moving to Caracas in 1928 to practise as an architect. His time in Paris was significant for reasons beyond his formal education; he was immersed in the city during an extraordinarily experimental period in art and architecture, and established lasting contacts there. His subsequent invitation to design the Venezuelan pavilion for the Paris Exposition Internationale des Arts et Techniques Appliques dans la Vie Moderne in 1937 brought him to the epicentre of art and architectural debate and in contact with a series of European architects, including Alvar and Aino Aalto, Le Corbusier, Robert Mallet-Stevens and Auguste Perret. He also engaged with artists including Pablo Picasso, Fernand Léger, Robert and Sonia Delaunay, Jean Arp and Sophie Taeuber-Arp, Joan Miró, László Moholy-Nagy and the American sculptor, Alexander Calder, many of whom he invited to contribute to his later projects, as well as accumulating their artwork for his own collection.

Villanueva led the major development for the University in Caracas, starting with a masterplan for the first phase in 1944–7. Paradoxically, the semi-feudal state of Venezuela provided exceptional opportunities at this time for large-scale public works, where the architect was afforded sovereignty over design decisions. By contrast, in democratic countries with a free-market economy, it would be much more difficult to achieve such a comprehensively co-ordinated outcome. In her book on Villanueva, Sibyl Moholy-Nagy stressed the importance of the social, economic and cultural context for Villanueva's work in South America. The scope and authority with which he was entrusted allowed him to make recommendations for contemporary artists of the highest international standing to be given a free hand, rather than pandering to the 'strangling interference of the lowest common design denominator'.[5] A series of artist acquaintances were invited to make artwork for site-specific locations across the central area of the campus, which was developed between 1952 and 1953. In the completed project, now listed as an UNESCO World Heritage Site, the art and architecture have become inseparable. Although each work was conceived by the artists autonomously, there is a conscious interrelationship between the artworks and the architecture.

Villanueva orchestrated the works as a promenade in such a way that staff, students and visitors would be exposed to art and vibrant colour along their daily routes. Decoration on the architecture was limited and Villanueva preferred to use a material-based palette of mass concrete and perforated block screens, with the deep shadows created by the tropical sun used to articulate the structure and form. Colour was injected by the artistic collaborations, such as a blue gable by the local Venezuelan painter Alejandro Otero on the architecture building, bronze in the sculptures and from artworks in mosaic and glass. Villanueva did not consider the artworks to be decorative in themselves but had an expectation that they would bring 'an explosion of colour in space'.[6] A covered route meanders between the various buildings, with the roof overhang held back in places. Sitting to one side between the 'Hall of Honor' and the Rectory block is a curved mosaic wall by Pascual Navarro in yellow, green, grey, black and white (fig.7.3). The murals were located in these clearings on free-standing curving walls and in full sun, but viewed from the cool deep shade. The contrast in light amplifies the intensity of the colour. Although

7.3 Carlos Raúl Villanueva, covered plaza with mosaic mural by Pascual Navarro, University of Caracas, 1953–4

he has been charged with a certain degree of post-rationalisation in his articulation of the experience of these encounters, the composition was clearly designed with the purpose of synthesising the art and architecture.

At a gathering space outside the main 'Aula Magna' auditorium, a sculpture, *Cloud Shepherd* by Jean Arp, sits in front of a curved screen wall with a mural by Mateo Manaure. Nearest the entrance to the hall is a tighter curved wall with an aluminium fin sculpture, *Positive-Negative* by Victor Vasarely; a free-standing *Amphion* sculpture by Henri Laurens then sits adjacent to a curved wall with mosaics on

both sides by Fernand Léger. Such was the unusual trust between Léger and the architect that he sent a note with his sketches to allow Villanueva to adjust the space between the elements of the composition 'for the best effect' in relation to both light and the distance of the viewer (fig.2.2).[7] Inside the Aula Magna at the culmination of the journey, Alexander Calder's acoustic panels are suspended above the auditorium. The floating forms introduce yellow, blue, red, orange, grey and black lozenges set against the main palette of wooden chairs, brown curtains, white walls and ceiling. The artwork is completely attuned to the spatial character of the

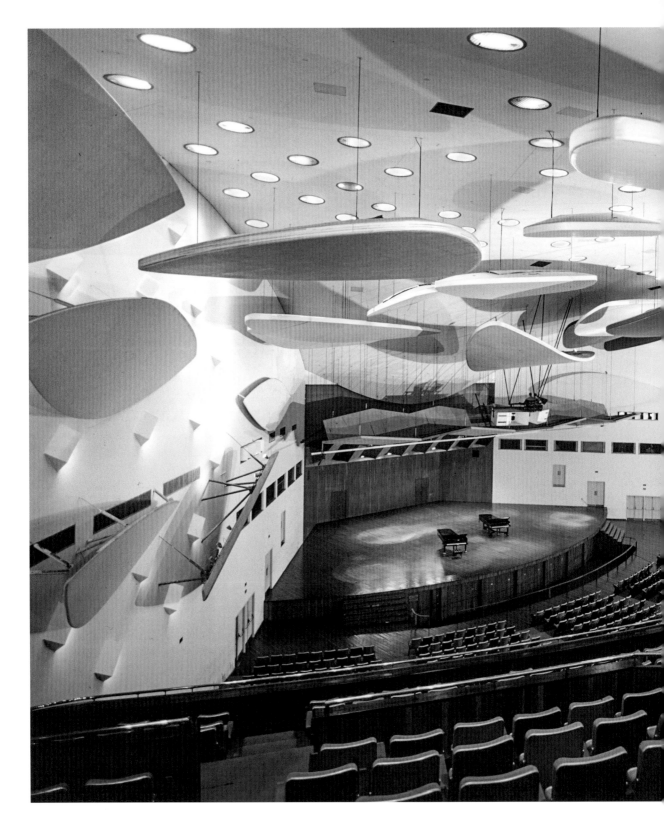

7.4 Alexander Calder, *Acoustic Ceiling*, 1954; Carlos Raúl Villanueva, Aula Magna auditorium, University of Caracas, 1953

hall, and inseparable as a modifier of the sensory experience through colour and sound quality (fig.7.4).[8]

Returning in 1954 to the theme of a synthesis of the arts, Villanueva defined the intended results of the collaborations as a 'new architectural-sculptural-pictorial organism, where none assumes a minor importance, where no fissure exists between all human aspirations'.[9] His stated aim was to instigate a process that would corroborate, accentuate or transform relationships between form and space.

In 1979, the architect Colin St John Wilson (1922–2007) penned a short article, 'Reflections on the Relation of Painting to Architecture'. The opening line bemoans the situation in the UK at that time, when there was no formal requirement for works of art to be commissioned in public buildings, although a footnote was added: 'The Arts Council is now sponsoring a scheme to advise in the financing of works of art in public buildings.'[10] St John Wilson was an avid art collector throughout his life, a friend to a wide range of artists, and he firmly believed that there was mutual benefit to collaboration, even though the general zeitgeist was less supportive. The essay cites remarks by the architect James Stirling and artist Mark Rothko that insisted on opposing positions, neither seeing any need for, nor benefit to be gained in siting art within architecture. St John Wilson was influential in his fight for the inclusion of many exceptional artworks within his own public buildings, notably R.B. Kitaj's tapestry and Eduardo Paolozzi's landmark sculpture at his British Library project in London (1962–98).

A similar campaign by the architect Eugene Rosenberg led to many successful collaborations, documented in his 1992 book, *Architect's Choice: Art in Architecture in Great Britain since 1945*.[11] Rosenberg argues that a key role for the architect is to act as instigator, patron and mediator to encourage clients to include a budget for artworks from the early stages of a building project. Like Villanueva and St John Wilson, Rosenberg was an art collector and he took every possible opportunity to persuade his clients to include an allowance for artwork. He is credited with securing Henry Moore's *Family Group* sculpture for Stevenage New Town in 1960, while Victor Pasmore's *Point of Contact* and Patrick Heron's paintings, *Orange and Lemon with White* and *Four Vermilions* were commissioned

7.5   Haworth Tompkins with Antoni Malinowski, Coin Street Neighbourhood Centre, London, 2007

7.6   Antoni Malinowski, painting in main stair at the Coin Street Neighbourhood Centre, London, 2007

for his own project at the University of Warwick in 1965. His driving force was to avoid situations in which public art was deposited randomly, with 'no viable connection' to the building.[12] One senses that his enthusiasm was infectious, encouraging clients to take a leap of faith to give space to artists, and to allowing a relatively free hand to develop work that was site-specific and challenging.

There is clearly a role for architects in persuading clients to include an artist as a collaborator, although some building typologies may lend themselves more readily than others because of the creative aspirations of the clients. The London-based architects Haworth Tompkins have built a reputation for cultural projects, notably for the performing arts. They clearly enjoy the involvement of artists in the development of their work, and in most cases it is the architects who have prompted collaboration, convincing the client of the important contribution that an artist can bring. Their 25-year collaboration with the visual artist Antoni Malinowski has produced a series of highly acclaimed theatre projects that are threaded through this book. Their architecture is firmly rooted in human sensory experience and has a richness that feels both comfortable and uplifting in use. In the theatres in particular, colour plays a significant role in creating the right atmosphere to shift the mood of the members of the audience, adjusting their mindset towards the performance. Steve Tompkins considers colour to be fundamentally about space and time, rather than as surface decoration. The metaphysical complexity of colour – ethereal and constantly shifting in appearance – is an essential tool for space-making and germane to the realisation of their buildings. Although the practice is clearly visually literate with colour, they readily acknowledge that Malinowski

adds a 'benign complexity to the design process and to the end result'.[13] Steve Tompkins notes that their collaborations always bring an additional dimension to the way in which the space develops, and the more so when the artist can participate in the studio discussions from an early stage.

During the design development of their Coin Street Neighbourhood Centre in London (2007), for example, Malinowski would be present in the architects' studio, working together on large-scale models to study the effect of colour in a void behind the facade, where saturated red and ultramarine blue are paired. The colour is less apparent by day but reveals itself through the facade at night (fig.7.5). Once the design principle was agreed, Tompkins stresses the importance of allowing an autonomy of practice, to trust and not 'tread too heavily in each other's territory'. Malinowski introduced a ceiling painting set at the top of the main in situ concrete stair, which gently softens the bare concrete finish (fig.7.6).

Most valuably, Haworth Tompkins have noted that artists 'problematise the design process', and

7.7   Page\Park Architects, ceramic tile facade, Leeds Playhouse, 2019

7.8   Rachel Duckhouse, Edinburgh Printmakers Entrance Gates (Page\Park Architects), 2019

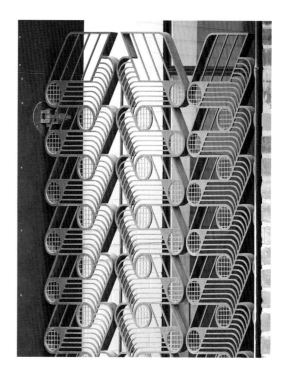

will 'quite rightly, refuse to simply go down the linear path of problem-solving'. This can make for an uncomfortable relationship at times if the working practices of the parties are at odds under the budget and programmatic pressures of delivering a building. An artist is likely to enlist a wider set of references to expand the conversation, and may unlock a spatial problem that may not have been identified as a problem. Although challenging, Haworth Tompkins suggest the reason they continue to work with artists including Clem Crosby, Nathan Coley, Victoria Morton and Martin Creed is that the result has greater richness and depth, and 'far more meaning'.[14] While this way of working might not suit a more self-centred context, Tompkins argues that his practice revels in a multiplicity of voices and different sensibilities.

The Glasgow-based architects Page\Park have worked on several restoration projects for the arts sector that have been developed through collaborative practices. In the renovation of the Leeds Playhouse (2019), it was the creative theatre company as client rather than a visual artist which seems to have encouraged the architects towards an expressed narrative and bolder use of colour than they might otherwise have employed (fig.7.7).[15] Although architects will develop a conceptual basis for each project, this may remain as an internal reference device for the practice and not be explicitly articulated through the architecture. At the Playhouse, however, the client's experience as 'professional storytellers' stimulated the architects' use of an expressed narrative. Four ceramic faience panels form the facade to a new public foyer that re-orientates the theatre to the street.[16] The lively 20-colour palette represents the four different characters of the four theatres within the building. Black tiles dispersed vertically on the towers

can be read as abstracted silhouettes of actors in the footlights. The colourful panels reflect the energetic, dynamic nature of the theatre company and have quickly become emblematic of the Leeds Playhouse's new lease of life. In 2007, Page\Park's renovation of the Eden Court Theatre (1976) in Inverness included several commissions for artists. Project architect Nicola Walls recalls that the collaboration with one artist, Donald Urquhart, was initially focused on an artwork, *Skyline Forms*, which wraps around five passive ventilation shafts, expressed as chimneys. The atmospheric artwork is an intense blue – 'the pure colour of a Scottish sky' – with highly polished stainless-steel panels to reflect the passage of the clouds and to make a visual connection to the function of the towers as devices for air movement. This initial commission led into a conversation with the architects that informed colour choices for the external render – a yellow from gorse bushes combined with a muted heather, derived from the local landscape. Working alongside the artist gave the architects the confidence to incorporate colour in a more meaningful manner.

At an early stage of their renovation of new premises for the Edinburgh Printmakers (2019), the clients developed an 'open call' for artists to respond to an outline brief for embedded artworks, with the project architect on the selection panel. The artist Rachel Duckhouse was selected for a set of sculptural gates on the main elevation (fig.7.8). Her work is characterised by her interest in lines, patterns and inter-connections generated as a way of articulating a particular field of enquiry. She had already completed a series of artist residencies – for example, *Shell Meets Bone* (2016/17), working with Professor Maggie Cusack at the University of Glasgow School of Geographical and Earth Sciences. Although such residencies could be interpreted as a form of artist-led collaborative practice, Duckhouse considers her work with scientists and other agencies, including architects, as a form of research that informs her artistic practice. For the artist, the commission for the Printmakers gates was a formative experience. Although the artwork had to modify and adapt in response to structural and legislative restrictions, she conceived it as 'a drawing', albeit one that materialised into dark, black-grey steel to match the window frames, and which subtly shifts in appearance with the angle of the sunlight.[17] Seen adjacent to the red brick, the colour appears tinged with green.

The dialogue was clearly fruitful for both parties. For the artist, a collaboration of this kind is a chance to develop their practice across different scales and materials, and to gain insights into other fields.[18] For Page\Park, as with most of the architects interviewed, their collaborative practices with artists have brought a fresh perspective to the design process, as well as an additional stratum of art and craft to the execution. This form of discourse has similarities with the process of 'Knowledge Exchange' in an academic context. Through artwork, the artist provides a non-textual expression of insights that might otherwise be unseen.

INTERMEDIARIES

If there is no established relationship between artist and architect, forging an arranged marriage between parties is unlikely to be straightforward

or successful, and where a client feels coerced to include artwork, it may be inappropriately sited and seen as an awkward afterthought. In 1987, Deanna Petherbridge edited *Art for Architecture: A Handbook on Commissioning*, based on the work of the publicly funded Art and Architecture Research Team and published in the form of guidance for commissioners by the UK Government Department of the Environment. At that time, there was a resurgence of interest in public art and clearly it was felt that there were lessons to be learnt. There was also a societal perception of the need for both art and architecture to be socially relevant and human-centric.[19] This would include a move towards traditional materials, craft and ornamentation. Furthermore, the book notes that for artists and sculptors, the opportunity to make work beyond the gallery setting might engage and challenge a wider public and give a 'sense of purpose'. In conducting interviews with contemporary artists for the book, a consistent theme to emerge was that it was an opportunity for them to reach a different audience beyond the hermetic world of the gallery.

Petherbridge's book provides a kind of 'how to' manual, complete with step-by-step flow charts and a range of model pathways defined as: 'The Perfect Patron', 'Artist-initiator', 'Advanced Architect-led' and the 'Complex Collaborative'. In terms of pitfalls, the handbook highlights a series of issues that do not appear to have abated. First, the author notes that 'commissions tend to be predictable, conventional and bland', and gives a nudge for patrons to take more risks and be more adventurous. Although much has changed since the handbook was published – most notably the gradual loss of architects employed in local government departments and a decline in public commissions – much of the advice on how to forge successful collaborations seems remarkably current. The introduction suggests that the coming together of artists and architects tends to run in parallel with periods of creative vitality; for example, the Renaissance, Baroque, Arts and Crafts, Bauhaus, post-war and, in the late 1980s (when the book was written), when postmodernism provided a background of pluralism in art and architecture. St John Wilson considered that a rift between art and architecture was firmly rooted in the Modern Movement and in divergence in fields of education. In wrestling with these two competing 'plastic arts', he wrote that architects 'firmly established a doctrine that the visual arts were not only subservient to architecture but could only be tolerated subject to very strict controls', with a corollary from artists 'with an equally strong belief in the sacrosanct nature of their own practice, and refusal to compromise it in any collaborative exercise'.[20] In 1989, the first meeting in 40 years between the Arts Council and the Royal Institute of British Architects (RIBA) discussed the dearth of opportunities for cross-fertilisation and fruitful contact, concluding that 'the general picture of mutual indifference is damaging to visual culture as a whole'.[21] Funding for public art in the UK has continued to ebb and flow, with notably successful schemes, such the Royal Society of Arts, Art for Architecture programme (1990–2003), but no consistent base line for funding. Clearly, there was a role for intermediaries to instigate and guide the various parties to a successful collaboration.

Today, international art commissioning agencies have emerged, as honest brokers, to assist in the pairing of artists with patrons, architects with artists. There is clearly a demand for artwork in architectural settings, yet many commissions are last-minute purchases to titivate a bland space, thus missing out on an opportunity for collaborative practice and truly site-specific work. Worse still, as artist Mark Titchner commented, is to be presented with an architectural render that has an image of 'art' pasted into the view. This is unsettling, reducing the role of the artist to someone commissioned to make a work that somehow fits the predetermined 'vision'. Although rare, such misunderstandings generate uncomfortable situations. Key lessons have been learnt and are now at the heart of good practice. Experienced art co-ordinators and commissioners – for example, Vivien Lovell, the founder of Modus Operandi – navigate these tensions daily. She recommends a written art strategy or policy to ensure that there is a firm understanding of the scope of the artwork, followed by a written brief before embarking on a process of longlisting, shortlisting, competitive interview or invited competition and selection. Ideally, the involvement of both client and architect should smooth the process. Lovell has continued to lobby for a UK policy change to formalise

the funding for art, as is commonplace in most European countries, the US and Canada.[22]

Ann Magnusson, a Swedish art commissioner with over 20 years of experience – and who commissioned Morag Myerscough for artwork in Linköping University Hospital – suggests that much of the tension that constantly occurs relates to a general sense of nervousness about the nature of art, perhaps through unfamiliarity or a feeling of loss of control.[23] Although a clear narrative can help to 'sell' the work to the various stakeholders, the essence of an artistic process is that the result is not entirely predictable or explicable in the way an architectural design is fully explored and justified in practical terms before execution. There is always an element of risk, but if the expectations are too tightly controlled, the chance for a responsive piece will be diminished. For example, Peter Lanyon's ceramic murals with architects Fry Drew Drake & Lasdun at the University Civil Engineering Building in Liverpool (1959) altered radically in both form and colour between the stage of his paper studies and the final work. Magnusson sees her role as 'making space for the artist', literally, to ensure that their work is not relegated to an inappropriate position, but more significantly, to make space in the conversation for the work to emerge. Some projects can allow for more of an open-ended brief to which artists can respond, especially if they have been involved at a stage while the architecture is evolving. An equivalent of an architect's 'concept design' stage can reduce the potential for unwanted surprises, and contracts should now include responsibilities for maintenance, repair and future decommissioning of the artwork. Paradoxically, the use of such contractual language may seem counter to the uncertainty, complexity and ambiguity that lies at the heart of art production, but it is intended to safeguard both artist and client. Antoni Malinowski's *Spectral Flip* painting in Oxford (2015) was commissioned by Vivien Lovell after the Mathematical Institute building by Viñoly was completed, but with the full knowledge and support of the architect and project architect (see figs 5.26 and 5.27). It is an example where there was an indication of the scope of the work, but the nature of the outcome of the artist's process (discussed in Chapter 5) could not have been predicted. Some sectors, such as culture, healthcare and education, are more receptive to an open-ended collaborative discussion, while other, commercial sectors may be more likely to commission an artwork after completion unless planning guidance stipulates integration of the artwork at an early stage. Where there is an opportunity for a collaborative practice to develop, a shared conceptual aim, with trust and generosity on all sides, seems vital to underpin any successful collaboration.

CREATIVE DISRUPTION THROUGH DIALOGUE

Occasionally, fruitful collaborations emerge from personal tensions, like grit in the oyster, a combination of opposites that becomes more than a mechanical means to produce a shared output. A relationship that is too abrasive or forced is, however, unlikely to succeed. Reflecting on why some collaborations are successful, Scottish

7.9   Bruce McLean and Will Alsop, Blizard Building, Queen Mary's University, London, 2005

sculptor, Bruce McLean (b. 1944) puts it succinctly: 'Big ego–big ego not a problem, easy peasy, big ego–small ego . . . a problem'.[24] From the outside looking in, his long-term collaboration with the architect Will Alsop (1947–2018) seems to have thrived on their unco-ordinated and spontaneous ebullience. There was an audaciousness to this partnership based on mutual respect and a friendship that allowed each space to be speculative, making work that was instinctive and generative – not necessarily with specific purpose – but never meaningless. In his book, *Will Alsop – The Noise*, Tom Porter provides insights into their distinctive double act. Both shared a love of colour and gestural forms that fed into their own diverse outputs. The Blizard Institute at Queen Mary's University campus in London (2005) is one built example of their collaboration (fig.7.9). McLean made coloured glass panels that are embedded into the rectangular building shell, while the vibrant interior includes a series of pod forms supported on angled legs, reminiscent of Alsop's earlier projects, the Peckham Library, London (2000) and the Sharp Centre for Design in Ontario, Canada (2004). In their case, perhaps a physical output was not the point; they were, rather, accomplices in creative thinking and with a shared love of colour.

An earlier collaboration between McLean and the architect David Chipperfield at the Arnolfini Gallery in Bristol (1987) seems, in retrospect, an unlikely combination. Chipperfield has since become known internationally for a muted, material-based palette and formal restraint. In Bristol, the expectation from both the client, Barry Barker, and the architect was that McLean would bring colour through his artwork to an otherwise achromatic space. Chipperfield also readily accepted McLean's choreography of the space using the bar counter and seats as stage props in his terrazzo installation, *A Place to Lean*. The artist sought to shift the behaviour of customers, perhaps to underscore the composure of the architectural container with a vital, bodily engagement using the objects themselves, as he had in his performance work and furniture sculptures made for a gallery show in 1987. The bar has since been renovated and the artwork removed, but despite such different approaches, the collaboration produced a unique and memorable space (fig.7.10).[25]

7.10 Bruce McLean, *A Place to Lean*, 1987, bar counter at the Arnolfini Gallery, Bristol, David Chipperfield, architect

7.11   Bruce McLean, *Grey Garden*, 2010, oil on canvas,
20 × 20 cm (7 ⅞ × 7 ⅞ in), Owner artist

McLean's passion for colour is a lifelong obsession, which was stimulated by his childhood in Glasgow and his architect father's books on Matisse and the Scottish colourist painters. His use of saturated colour in both easel paintings– for example, *Grey Garden* (2010) (fig.7.11) – and in architectural settings is immediately affective and, like all colour, its use may appear simple but requires both skill and courage, particularly at the scale of architectural interventions. As the art critic Mel Gooding observed: 'colour was crucial in freeing McLean' as '. . . a means by which space and atmosphere could be created in two dimensions and the convulsions of social behaviour depicted without irrelevant recourse to perspective and modelling'.[26]

For McLean, the significance of interdisciplinary dialogue was instilled through his experience of teaching at the Croydon School of Art (1968–71) as part of a short-lived, but innovative, foundation course which brought him together with artists, an environmental psychologist, a composer and an ergonomicist. The intersubjective nature of the

course was stimulating, positively encouraging a collaborative approach that has stayed with him. Will Alsop was both painter and architect, and McLean – who describes himself as a sculptor who paints – clearly also enjoys moving between a wide range of material practices – performance, easel painting, wall paintings, ceramics, enamelling, glass – and between small-scale, large-scale, permanent and temporary works. This agility also underscores his approach to art and architecture, and in the best works there is no distinction or boundary between disciplines. In this he refers to his Glasgow roots and his love of the dexterity of Charles Rennie Mackintosh who, in common with Gio Ponti and other notable 20th-century architects, worked between painting, furniture, ironmongery and architecture. McLean is frustrated that there are few opportunities to work in a truly collaborative manner with architects from an early stage in the design. More often he will be invited in at a late stage with a restricted brief. For a commission at the Coventry University Hospital, for example, McLean made a massive wall painting, *A Healing Garden* (2006), that envelops the upper walls of the curving foyer space with vivid blue, yellow, green, red, magenta and black plywood shapes reminiscent of Matisse 'cut-outs'. The plant forms are unconstrained by the spatial dimensions, appearing to creep out of the frame to draw attention to the architectural space and to lift the gaze upwards (fig.7.12).

In less successful examples, he cites poor communication between parties, or a lack of empathy that undermined the relationships. McLean has, on occasion, been invited to work within buildings that are not strong architecturally and if there is little contact with the end-users during the process, there can be issues with the treatment of artwork that may be seen as solely decorative. Although – in common with the other artists interviewed – he is sanguine about the longevity of embedded artwork, it can be soul-destroying to see a gas pipe thoughtlessly drilled through, or posters peppered over, a considered artwork.

As with Alsop and McLean, beneficial collaborations between artists, architects and other parties may be focused on intellectually stimulating dialogues – as a sounding board, to counsel, to embolden or to invite creative disruption. The Swiss architects Herzog & de Meuron acknowledge that

7.12　Bruce McLean, *A Healing Garden*, 2006, paint on wall and formed plywood, Coventry University Hospital Foyer

conversations with artists need not necessarily result in an active involvement or even a physical output. Rather than trying to see things in the same way, it seems vital to successful collaborations that there is a difference in the angle of curiosity and a different analytical approach. Herzog & de Meuron value the scrutiny of simple assumptions and design decisions. For example, Jacques Herzog cites the decision process involved in establishing the size of the leaf motif that wraps around the surface of

their Ricola project in Mulhouse, France (1993).[27] The architects had been pursuing the idea of a printed facade for a competition for the library at the Jussieu Campus in Paris, in collaboration with the German artist Gerhard Richter (1992) whose use of the serial photographic image is a constant thread in his *Atlas* work.[28] Although that project was not realised, the idea had been seeded and was carried into the Mulhouse project, which was being developed at the same time. Despite having an established concept, achieving the right scale of the pattern for the extensive landscape of the surface was vital. For the Ricola project, the architects consulted another artist ally, Rémy Zaugg (1943–2005), and through a sinuous conversation, an appropriate size was established. For their Eberswalde Technical School Library (1999) the concept was developed further with photographic newspaper images, catalogued by the artist Thomas Ruff, etched into precast concrete panels and screen-printed onto glass. The effect is such that Catherine Hürzeler suggests that 'the body of the building can no longer be distinguished from the pictorial surface'.[29] The architects are known to approach each project in a unique way, allowing undercurrents of thought to ferment, piqued by evolving conversations in the company of artists. The outcome for the artist appears not to be predictable, varying from a brief consultation to an interdependent design. Hürzeler surmises that Herzog & de Meuron's aim is not specifically to 'incorporate art into their architecture', but rather to find a new language by uniting their architecture with art.[30]

This open-minded approach is also evident in an emboldened use of colour for the Laban Dance Centre in London (2003), where Herzog & de Meuron worked with the artist Michael Craig-Martin. Craig-Martin has made a substantial number of permanent artworks within architectural settings, some collaboratively, some as commissions. In his collaborations he brings experiential knowledge of colour to the fore. Decisions on colour are never easy, but a deep understanding of the phenomenological effects that an artist may have wrestled with for many years is a key reason for inviting an artist to participate in the architect's dialogue. The Laban project, situated in what was then a nondescript docklands site to the east of the city, won the UK Stirling Prize for architecture (2003). The choice of colours used – bright green, turquoise and magenta – is unlike anything else by the architects, and is clearly influenced by the artist (fig.7.13). Colour is used in three different ways within the project – directly on surfaces, by diffusion, and by reflectance. The building is deceptively complex, with a simple external form enclosing a labyrinth of a plan and section. Within this spatial network, the three main pathways are differentiated by colour. The use of block colour acts as a wayfinding device, but also shifts the feeling of each route. The hue is saturated but with a touch of white to lift the tone. The second use of colour is very subtle, as a pale tint in the translucent polycarbonate cladding. Craig-Martin likens the effect to oil on water, perhaps a reference to the adjacent disused docks. For the dancers inside the studios, the colour had to be soft and diffused to avoid distraction, but it is allowed to leak into the interiors. During the day, the highly polished floor surfaces bounce the light, further dispersing the reflected colour. For some critics, the use of colour at the Laban is overly dominant, tipping the architects out of their comfort zone, but for users of the building, the slightly dissonant colour is completely integral to the architecture and sense of place.

A large wall painting by Craig-Martin wraps the main theatre space and becomes a memorable landmark, combined with the tilting ground plane (fig.7.14). His abstracted everyday objects are immediately recognisable and he redeploys the

7.13   Herzog & de Meuron, colour and diffused light, Laban Dance Centre, London, 2003, with Michael Craig-Martin

same set of objects from a taxonomy gathered over many years.[31] They are used at various enlargements, frequently in tension with the architectural surface. The objects clash with doors and wrap as they turn a corner. While finding the right scale for their leaf motif became an obsession for the architects at Ricola, here the scale of the object is entirely controlled by the artist to accentuate the tension. Had this been a decorative application, one suspects that great care would have been taken to ensure that a pattern would fit comfortably, but the artwork does the opposite. It becomes a way of engaging with and enhancing the architectural surface. For Craig-Martin, it was the act of making a large-scale installation in 1993 that became pivotal in his own work, so in effect he came to his easel painting because of an architectural scale installation, rather than the other way around.[32]

As at Villanueva's University of Caracas campus, the Laban Dance Centre demonstrates a unity of art and architecture that are inseparable as a total artwork. In each case, the dynamic balance

between autonomous art and architecture has established a productive tension. This is not art added to embellish bland architecture: the reason these schemes are successful is that the architecture is also resonant and conceptually strong. The art and architecture, born out of a fruitful collaborative practice, are combined to invigorate the sensory experience of space. To invite an artist like Bruce McLean is to invite a piercing wit that may be disconcerting to some, that may challenge working practices to breaking point, but brings with it a way of seeing, and a way of working freely with colour that gives an immediate and enduring pleasure. According to Jane Rendell in *Art and Architecture: A Place Between*, successful collaboration between artists and architects relates less to disciplinary distinctions and more to how individuals work together in a self-aware manner 'towards end points that are decided through mutual consent'.[33] The potential for disruption to orthodox practices offers each party a shift in perspective, particularly in working with colour.

7.14 Michael Craig-Martin, *Laban Wall Drawing*, 2003, Herzog & de Meuron, Laban Dance Centre, London

8 Constructing the Inseparable

A House for Essex: The Philosopher, The Artist, The Architect and The Public

This final chapter aims to synthesise the main themes of the book through one specific example, *A House for Essex*, where artwork is so fully integrated into architecture that both have become fused together. The project provides insights into the interrelationship of art and architecture, artists and architects, the significance and spatial dynamics of colour, light and shadow, human experience and engagement, perception and movement, and collaborative practices.

Schloss Charlottenhof at Potsdam, designed by the architect Karl Friedrich Schinkel (1826–9) and discussed in Chapter 3, brought together, as 'A Collaboration in Arcadia', a number of individual characters who have left us an extraordinary piece of architecture that is interlaced with intellectual rigour and allegorical readings of light and dark and of natural cycles of life and death. It employs colour in a painterly manner as part of a promenade that also reaches out into the gardens beyond. In Iain Boyd Whyte's essay on the Schloss Charlottenhof, he identifies four protagonists – an informed client, an architect, a landscape designer and a writer.[1] It seems that the combination of these individuals, their skills and obsessions, became intertwined to produce a modest building, but one which, when further investigated, challenges the audience with enduring and universal themes. *A House for Essex*, which was completed in 2014, could not be more different in terms of its outward expression, but plays with similarly profound and moving motifs. It is highly decorative, garishly colourful and attention-grabbing. The small building – which is presented to the world as simultaneously an artwork and a holiday home, is the product of a constellation of characters, real and fictitious. Here, the four parties to be introduced are: The Philosopher, The Artist, The

Architect and The Public. We will consider these in turn and their contribution to this unique project.

The philosopher is the writer Alain de Botton, who was the initial client at the instigation of this project. In founding 'Living Architecture' in 2006, his aim was to reach a wider audience than is possible through the written word. Although his books – notably in this context, *The Architecture of Happiness* (2006) – have been influential within a hermetic audience, he was aware that to some extent he was effectively preaching to the converted.[2] He came to the realisation that by commissioning physical buildings by internationally acclaimed architects for short-term holiday lets, the public might have a first-hand experience of thought-provoking architecture. All of the houses are in the UK, set in very carefully chosen sites. The series is eclectic – a materially rich villa made of hand-rammed concrete set into rolling countryside in Devon by the Swiss architect Peter Zumthor; NORD Architects' simple black house in the coastal shingles wilderness of Dungeness (with the filmmaker Derek Jarman's house and garden nearby); the *Balancing Barn* by the Dutch practice MVRDV; John Pawson's minimal *Life House*; and others by Michael and Patti Hopkins, Jarmund/ Vigsnæs Architects and David Kohn with artist Fiona Banner. Stylistic taste, if there is such a thing, is not the driver behind the series. No particular architectural approach is favoured. Each house is connected to its site in a meaningful manner and has a strength of concept and rigour in the delivery of the architectural idea made physical. Most of the projects are architect-led. The closest contemporary example in commissioning high-profile architects to create a series of buildings in the UK is the Maggie's Cancer Care Centres instigated by Charles Jencks,

8.1 Grayson Perry/FAT Architecture, *A House for Essex*, 2014

who, like Alain de Botton, is also a writer and an informed client. In commissioning *A House for Essex*, De Botton took a leap of faith and substantial risk in pairing the artist Grayson Perry with the architect Charles Holland, then of FAT Architecture (Fashion Architecture Taste) (fig.8.1).[3]

De Botton's connection to the artist preceded the commission. They had previously discussed the making of a large-scale artwork in the form of a small secular chapel, but this had never been realised. De Botton was born in Switzerland and had memories of a considered domestic architecture that was not typically replicated in the UK. The tradition of the European single-family house is not readily available to British architects as a typology in the same way, partly because land ownership is so radically different. By making the focus a series of dwellings, De Botton's goal was to allow people to experience what an unconventional house might be. A holiday house brings with it a need for escape, for a change, for something both functionally ordinary and everyday, but which

also has the excuse of being out of the ordinary, refreshing and invigorating, or calm and reflective. The series of houses so far all have a sense of escape and inward reflection, and allow people to take a pause from their daily lives – and none more so than the collaboration between Perry, Holland and De Botton at Wrabness in Essex.

A House for Essex has more than one client. Exceptionally, it has an imaginary client conjured up by the artist as part of the narrative of the artwork. Rob, the second husband of Julie Cope, who is the central character in the story, emerges as the fictional client for a mausoleum – a 'Taj Mahal on the River Stour' – to celebrate the life of his dead wife. The aim here is not to repeat the narrative of the artwork, as it is fully recounted through a poem by the artist, *The Ballad of Julie Cope*, in a series of four large tapestries and other artefacts, and in numerous press articles and videos. It is essential, nevertheless, to understand the nature of the artwork as one ingrained in social and cultural observation through a pictorial narrative of the life of an ordinary woman

8.2   Grayson Perry/FAT Architecture, *A House for Essex*, bedroom interior with Julie Cope tapestry by Perry

from the sometimes maligned English county of Essex – Julie Cope. Architects are accustomed to working for and with a client, but not a fictional one. Yet the client is one of the protagonists in the making of the artwork – her life and taste was channelled by both artist and architect as part of decision-making and design development (fig.8.2).

The artist is Grayson Perry, who is a highly popular and internationally known ceramicist, who won the UK's prestigious Turner Prize in 2003. He moves fluidly across a range of disciplines and identities, including cross-dressing into Claire, his female alter ego. Perry has likened the many identities that we all possess as akin to the strands of colour that lie along the back of a tapestry. While multiple colours are present, giving the fabric a thickness and complexity, some come to the surface along the way, retreat, then reappear again.[4] Unlike many contemporary artists who have studio assistants, Perry makes all of his own artwork. This paradox of multiple personas bound within a singular individual was also a factor in the collaborative nature of *A House for Essex*. Perry was introduced to Holland by their non-fictional client, Alain de Botton, in an uncomfortable encounter that very nearly derailed the collaboration at the outset.[5] Perry had a distrust of architects in general, concerned that they lacked his vivacity and that contemporary architecture was similarly anaemic and dull. For Perry, however, the project provided an intriguing opportunity to work on a large scale, enduring, complex three-dimensional piece, and to reach a wider social audience than would be likely to visit a gallery show.

The architect is Charles Holland, who might appear as a counterbalance to Perry's exuberance. Within the profession of architecture, however, his practice was considered to be avant-garde, undoubtedly running against the tide of restrained neo-modernism and the 'New London' calm brick aesthetic that was becoming prevalent at the time. The practice, FAT Architecture, formed by architects Sam Jacob, Sean Griffiths and Holland, came to the fore through their housing projects for the developer Urban Splash in Manchester. They looked to Robert Venturi and Denise Scott Brown as well as to Edwin Lutyens, Adolf Loos and John Soane, to neo-Baroque and Mannerist architecture. The practice's work was knowingly eclectic,

8.3   FAT Architecture, *Blue House*, London, 2002

employing both colour and decorative elements. The *Blue House* (2002), designed by Sean Griffiths (who was both client and architect), is a celebrated example of their work that combines a house and office behind a sculpted billboard (fig.8.3). For the architects, the Living Architecture project in Essex was one of their last works before the practice disbanded in 2014. Holland has since set up his own practice and combines teaching, writing and research alongside architecture and design. All of the partners continue to use colour in a confident manner in their work.

Finally, with any project or artwork there is the audience. The appetite for art by internationally acclaimed artists of the standing of Grayson Perry can be voracious. He is caught between art collectors hungry for investments, his scepticism of 'made for gallery' work, and his own constrained capacity to make the art. In this case, the celebrity status of the artist himself has elevated

8.4 and 8.5　Grayson Perry/
FAT Architecture, *A House for
Essex* – view with summer
cornfields and detail of exterior
cast terracotta tlles

the level of interest in the work, and the nature and colourfulness of the artwork stirred public controversy in its rural setting. The success of the project in the media has caused problems with the number of visitors to the small community and impacted on the privacy of the paying guests in the house, who may feel besieged. This intensity of interest will subside over time, but the project has already morphed from house to pilgrimage site. Like a folly, one can imagine its future life as a beautiful ruin, or full of hay like Palladio's Villa Foscari La Malcontenta, for many centuries before it was renovated and its frescoes discovered and restored. In its present function, the immediate audience for *A House for Essex* are the visitors who rent the house and can spend time with the art, challenged to contemplate and internalise some of the profound narrative of life and death.

Although the audience may need time to dissect the overtly eclectic expression of the architecture, the impact of colour is immediate and fully integrated throughout the design. Externally the colour palette is dark green, white, gold and red. The gold roof, made from a copper and zinc alloy, is visible at a great distance (fig.8.4). The colour is supportive of the reading of the building as a wayside chapel, reminiscent of icon paintings and gilded domes, but the house also nestles into the gold of the adjacent summer cornfields. Faience tile cladding in green and white has a long tradition in the UK. Hendrik Berlage used green-glazed tiles at Holland House (1916), an early steel-framed structure in London, and Eric Parry Architects have used speckled green ceramic fins in the extension to the Holburne Art Gallery in Bath (as discussed in Chapter 5). White faience produced by the Burmantofts Pottery in Leeds was used at the iconic Michelin House in London (1911), although white-glazed tiles are more commonly used in tight backstreets or light wells to bounce light into adjacent windows. An advantage of the cast tile is its potential for pattern through repetition and sculpted relief to modulate light and shadow across the surface undulations. Ceramic tiles are also an exceptionally durable way of embedding colour on a surface, and as confirmed by Otto Wagner's floreate Majolica House in Vienna (1898), they are unlikely to fade in the sun. At *A House for Essex*, although acting as the cladding to basic concrete

block walls, the tiles are formally classed as 'artwork'. Grayson Perry made a series of tile designs depicting Julie, among other everyday objects symbolic of her life – a music tape, a nappy pin and so forth – which were cast at the Darwen Terracotta works (fig.8.5). Finally, deep red windows and doors contrast in hue with the green and gold.

The architect cites the practice's interest in both Adolf Loos and John Soane as part of the conceptual use of colour in their work. Adolf Loos's Müller House in Prague, recently renovated to restore the original colour scheme, is an acknowledged inspiration for its simplicity of design and use of colour in the domestic areas. Although from the outside, the axial form of the Essex house suggests a symmetrical promenade, internally it is asymmetrically arranged, with the sequence of spaces, hidden and revealed in stages. As in Venturi and Scott Brown's work, inside and outside are intentionally mismatched, unlike modernist houses that place a priority on transparency and fluidity. The project has an additive plan, with each room discrete from the next. Mirrors are set into doors alter the perception of space, and provide dramatic moments when opened to reveal an unexpected adjacent space, a device also used by Schinkel and Soane. At *A House for Essex*, mirrored doors face to the kitchen and bedrooms – defining the transition point between the front and back of the house, between the everyday of domestic areas and the sudden volume of the secular chapel/sanctuary. At this one point the spaces open into each other in section, with a minstrel's balcony placed either side to offer a high-level perspective from the bedrooms into the living space below (fig.8.6).

A strong yellow and red are used on the kitchen units and bedroom furniture, and the green ceramic tiles reappear internally in the hearth and upstairs bathroom (fig.8.7). In the upper front room of Soane's house at Lincoln's Inn Fields in London, a strong yellow is used with Pompeian red and green in the room below. Soane's houses continue to act as a reference for many contemporary architects, not only for his use of light and colour, but for the intensity of the spatial experience, of changing vistas, ambiguity and complexity.[6] Colour is further incorporated through floor patterns and a mosaic artwork in the vestibule. Walls in the bedrooms are white, both prosaic but also gallery-like, giving due attention to Perry's massive full colour tapestries that hang, one in each bedroom. The atmosphere of the main, double-height 'chapel' is starkly different. It is intended to be the most introspective space. With no low-level windows, it is darker at the base of the volume and is more contemplative in nature. It is reminiscent of the similarly intense, inward-looking, tall and top-lit mausoleum space at the Soane Museum in London. Painted in a dark grey, this top-lit space changes constantly with the light conditions. The space is warmed by the yellow sofas, the deep red woodwork on a central 'altarpiece' screen wall, and by two further large tapestries. The choice of hues has a dynamic effect. The red woodwork makes the adjacent grey appear greenish; the yellow seats will push it towards a blueish tone.

The use of saturated hues on the surfaces of the house resonates with the colour and detail in the artwork. It is therefore set in tension with the architecture and has to compete in a way that would not be the case if displayed in a gallery. While the architecture is a vessel for Perry's artwork, the boundary between art and architecture is less clear as they are mutually dependent. In the Residenz in Würzburg, Tiepolo's great ceiling and Balthasar Neumann's architecture are in balance. Neither dominates the other; both have an autonomy but are interdependent as the total work of art. At *A House for Essex*, the 'artwork' is catalogued for the visitor as a list in an accompanying pamphlet. The list includes each separate external tile design, the tapestries, pots and figures. The architecture is also discussed, its meanings and references offered as a way to access the curiosities of the compositions; but the artwork seems to have been carefully identified as autonomous to the architecture. It is ascribed a different status in terms of the perception of its present value as art. In terms of financial value, therefore, a dividing line has been drawn between art and architecture.

A number of commentators have applied the German term, *Gesamtkunstwerk*, to the house. It is clear that this is a rare, contemporary example of a total work of art. Yet, as noted in the preceding chapter, the term is more commonly used to describe a work by a single architect, such as Charles Rennie Mackintosh or Gio Ponti, in which the design of the building, furniture, cutlery, light fittings, rugs and all finishes are conceived in their entirety as a piece. *A House for Essex* is different. It has been co-created and is inseparable as a composition. It is also a rare example because of the difficulty in finding an equilibrium in this asymmetrical balance between the parts and the whole. It has a highly charged and sometimes knowingly awkward synthesis of parts to the whole, while at the same time allowing an intellectual space for each discipline. Grayson Perry's work is intensely crafted and he loves to wallow in the detail of the narrative. In places, therefore, the architecture hangs back and becomes simpler, but never mute. In terms of personalities, the start of the relationship between the parties was fraught and tensions were evident. There was risk on the part of all the protagonists, including the contractors and craftspeople involved in the construction. Trust and respect were far from guaranteed but slowly developed, as did a mutual understanding of the making of the work as socially and culturally significant. Issues of social class and taste are integral to the artwork and in the bold use of colour, and is a central theme of both architect and artist. There is a richness to the project in the way it leaps forwards and backwards between historical references, and a fluidity between its multiple identities similar to the artist him/herself. Perry's self-expressed aim in making his art is to get under people's radar, to allow his unconscious to talk to their unconscious. As a piece of architecture, it is designed to stimulate human intellectual and sensory experience through a series of uplifting spaces that are ordered, proportioned and constructed to have emotional resonance. Ultimately, together with their real and imaginary clients, the creators of *A House for Essex* have succeeded in collaborating to make a sophisticated addition to contemporary material culture that appears to be enjoyed by a wide audience.

TOP

8.6 Grayson Perry/FAT Architecture, *A House for Essex*, interior main space

BOTTOM

8.7 Grayson Perry/FAT Architecture, *A House for Essex*, interior domestic space

9.1 Mark Bradford, *We The People*, 2017, mixed media on canvas, 1219.2 × 2438.4 cm (480 × 960 in), 32 panels

9   Reflections on Art in Architecture

Mark Bradford's monumental work, *We The People* (2017), is positioned in the main entrance to the US Embassy (designed by KieranTimberlake Architects) in London. Its massive scale immediately demands attention. In an otherwise chromatically restrained space, the colour (small flecks of red and blue, some saturated, some muted into pink and blue-grey) draws attention to the words carved into the surface. The eye leads the mind to scan across the complex layered surface, which reveals its colour through erratic tears and erosions, searching for meaning. Although the work was made off-site, it is effectively embedded in the building, not only because of its scale, but more significantly through a critique of the very purpose of the architecture (fig.9.1). Jane Rendell suggests that by taking art out of the gallery setting, 'the parameters that define it are called into question and all sorts of new possibilities for thinking about the relationship between art and architecture are opened up'.[1] She elaborates that art can act as a form of 'critical spatial practice' that engages in social and political issues to question dominant ideologies. Bradford's work, quoting the US Constitution, challenges its architectural setting that could otherwise be read as mute, to render an explicit expression of its purpose. Together, art and architecture have become psychologically resonant and memorable as a place.

Within the architectural profession, there has been a nervousness in using colour in a strategic manner, and as an integrated part of the design process, perhaps as a result of the limited teaching of colour in contemporary architectural education. This timidity appears to be more than a simple lack of confidence with colour, however, and the idea 'that architecture is conceptually, if not literally white' has become deeply rooted.[2] While this appears to be changing, the results are often poorly executed and overly reliant on arbitrary choices

based on hue. Colour may be further restricted by the pre-determined range of product availability, which is further curtailed by material manufacturing processes and budget. As architecture should afford a sensual experiential engagement with its users, this book has argued that within this realm, colour is a fertile ground for collaborative constructive practice. Architects who have forged successful collaborations often seem to revel in the different perspective and critical interpretation of an artist, while artists exploit the infinite scale and complexity of colour, tone, texture and depth.

The reasons why there are relatively few examples of truly collaborative practice are worthy of further examination. A key issue is time. From interviews with both artists and architects, it is evident that good colour design, or the inclusion of art within architecture, benefits from a period of gestation. This itself is a major restriction, with design time squeezed in most construction programmes. Adding into the mix an artist, who may question and challenge decision-making, is risky. Collaborative activities extend the investment by all parties, demand the acquisition of new knowledge as part of the exchange, and may involve a process of experimentation and testing. The outcome is uncertain – much more so than an autonomous studio-produced artwork. Although the processes, contingencies and interdependencies of embedded artwork are complex in comparison to work for galleries, the opportunity to develop work that negotiates and responds to restraint and restriction seems to be welcomed by artists.

Reflecting on a renewed convergence between art and architecture, it is the potential to create resonance, sensorially and intellectually, that emerges as a common thread. For artists, it is not only scale and complexity of surfaces afforded by making site-specific work that is appealing, but perhaps most significantly, they consider work in architectural settings as engaging different audiences, at different levels of consciousness. Although the work may be seen in the peripheral vision, encountered by an inattentive audience, it can make a profound contribution to the experience of space. While there is a growth in contemporary spatial art, situated very precisely within found architectural settings and offering a radical critique, these works are normally restricted to short-lived installations. Artworks that are purchased as an afterthought, and deposited randomly without viable reference to their context, are also unlikely to find resonance. Discussions with professional art commissioners provide insights into practices that are designed to safeguard all parties and, most significantly, to use their experience and expertise to create a space for art. In long-term alliances, or where an artist can be involved from an early stage, there is scope for reciprocity to develop as an extended conversation that emboldens both parties. Such transactional exchanges do not suggest, however, that one activity should merge into the other, thereby lessening the distinction between disciplines. A logical development is contemporary multi-disciplinary art and architecture practices that provide physical co-working environments, varied voices, experiences, education and skills.[3]

These suggest loose alliances that may coalesce around making work with and for communities, or formal collaborative commissions.

This book has assumed that architecture, in common with art, necessitates an intellectual, conceptual approach that is always essentially synthetic, emerging in response to diverse influences. However, from the interviews conducted for this book, architects and artists do think and operate very differently. While the introduction, 'Spatial Synchronicity', began with a search for a harmonious constellation of built work and artistic enquiry, what has become apparent is a more agile and nuanced goal. In the final part, 'Constructing the Inseparable', this book argues against any attempt to bridge the gap, but rather emphasises that divergent approaches between the protagonists are, in themselves, valuable. From the first example of Giotto's frescoes, supported by the deep blue vault of the Arena Chapel in Padua, to Grayson Perry's pots and tapestries in *A House for Essex*, the examples given are deliberately eclectic. While a total work of art, or *Gesamtkunstwerk*, seeks homogeneity, collaborative practice engages a multiplicity of ways of thinking, tensions and dissonance that are productive. Although such an approach carries an element of risk, the examples provided suggest that it is possible to find a point of equilibrium where art and architecture are interdependent, yet inconceivable apart.

Notes

1   INTRODUCTION: SPATIAL SYNCHRONICITY

1   Richard Wright, quoted at https://www.the moderninstitute.com/exhibitions/scottish-national-gallery-of-modern-art-edinburgh-2010-06/4858/, accessed 19 February 2022.

2   Fiona Macpherson, 'Novel Colour Experiences', in Derek Brown and Fiona Macpherson (eds), *The Routledge Handbook of Philosophy of Colour*, Abingdon, Routledge, 2021, p.198.

3   Juhani Pallasmaa, 'Hapticity and Time: Notes on Fragile Architecture', in Juhani Pallasmaa and Peter MacKeith (eds), *Encounters 1: Architectural Essays*, Helsinki, Rakennustieto, 2012, p.331.

4   Remy Golan, *Muralnomad: The Paradox of Wall Painting, Europe 1927–1957*, New Haven, CT and London, Yale University Press, 2009, p.57.

2   SURFACE TENSIONS

1   Tess Jaray, *Painting: Mysteries and Confessions*, London, Royal Academy of Arts, 2012, pp 32–3.

2   David Leatherbarrow and Mohsen Mostafavi, *Surface Architecture*, Boston, MA, MIT Press, 2002, p.31.

3   Joseph Amato, *Surfaces: A History*, Berkeley, CA and London, University of California Press, 2013, p.17.

4   James J. Gibson, *An Ecological Approach to Visual Perception*, first published 1979, repr., New York, The Psychology Press, 2014, p.19.

5   Walter Benjamin, *The Rainbow: A Dialogue on Phantasy* (1915), as discussed in Howard Caygill, *Walter Benjamin: The Colour of Experience*, London, Routledge, 1998, p.10.

6   Willi Baumeister, quoted in Eduardo Westerdahl, *Willi Baumeister*, Santa Cruz de Tenerife, Ediciones Gaceta de Arte, 1934, noted at https://willi-baumeister.org/en/content/law-tables-art-willi-baumeisters-wall-pictures, accessed 15 July 2021.

7   Fernand Léger, 'Revival of Mural Art', in *The Listener*, vol.18, no.459, 25 August 1937, pp 408–9, repr. in Katia Baudin (ed.), *Fernand Léger: Painting in Space*, Cologne, Museum Ludwig / Munich, Hirmer Verlag, 2016, pp 132–3.

8   Giuliana Bruno, *Surface: Matters of Aesthetics, Materiality, and Media*, Chicago, IL and London, University of Chicago Press, 2014, p.187.

9   The assistants were trained to make the marks with a hard pencil worked in two directions across the surfaces. There will be differences evident in the minute movements of each hand, but sufficient similarities learned through training. The work was commissioned as part of a major renovation with architects Caruso St John. Artist Richard Wright was also commissioned to make a new window which uses a variety of textures of clear glass.

10   Svetlana Alpers and Michael Baxendall, *Tiepolo and the Pictorial Intelligence*, New Haven, CT and London, Yale University Press, 1994.

11   ibid., p.3.

12   ibid., p.107.

13   The architect Rachel Simmonds, of Smith Scott Mullan, suggested the idea of commissioning a contemporary artist when a large section of the original dome had to be replastered. See Rachel Simmonds, 'The King's Theatre', *The Magazine of the Architectural Heritage Society of Scotland*, Autumn 2013, pp 24–7. The work is also documented in a film directed by Lindsey Douglas for the BBC. John Byrne was assisted by a team of artists: Kevin Leary, Celie Byrne, Marion Curle, Fraser Gray, Gayle Bray and Stef Gardiner.

14   Essay by Mo Enright in Gimpel Fils (ed.), *Peter Lanyon: The Mural Studies*, London, Gimpel Fils Gallery, 1996.

15   Antonio Foscari, *Frescos within Palladio's Architecture: Malcontenta 1557–1575*, Zurich, Lars Müller Publishers, 2013.

16   ibid., p.9.

17   Eric Alliez and Jean-Claude Bonne, 'Matisse in the Becoming-Architecture of Painting', in Edward

Whittaker and Alex Landrum (eds), *Painting with Architecture in Mind*, Bath, Wunderkammer Press and Bath School of Art and Design, 2012, pp 38–70.

18 The Bauhaus was established by Walter Gropius in 1919 to integrate art, science and technology. Key figures in colour teaching were Johannes Itten, Paul Klee, Wassily Kandinsky and Josef Albers. Itten's book, *The Art of Color: The Subjective Experience and Objective Rationale of Color*, and Albers' *Interaction of Color*, were written much later in their lives in the 1960s and remain seminal texts for colour design. Both advocated experimentation, placing practice before theory.

19 Mark Pimlott, 'Natural Antagonism: Notes on Colour or Architecture', in Whittaker and Landrum (eds), *Painting with Architecture in Mind*, p.23.

20 ibid., p.24.

21 The paintings were sold as an artwork and were reconstructed in the Museum Haus Konstructiv in Zurich in 2016.

22 Malinowski established himself as an artist in London following a show of paintings at the Camden Arts Centre in 1997 and Gimpel Fils Gallery in 1999. Originally from Warsaw in Poland, he studied at the Academy of Fine Arts in Warsaw and the Chelsea College of Art, London. His material practice is discussed in Chapter 5, and his ongoing collaboration with Haworth Tompkins is further discussed in Chapter 7.

23 The metallic paint is Lascaux Copper Studio Bronze acrylic; the painting is conceived as a two-dimensional chandelier, immediately over the entrance.

24 Antoni Malinowski, from an interview with the author, London, 2019.

3 ARCHITECTS AS SPATIAL PAINTERS

1 Pompeii had been discovered in 1549 by Domenico Fontana, but then covered over until 1748 when it was first excavated. Schinkel made his visit to Pompeii around 1804.

2 According to Arthur Rüegg, this was for cost reasons; see Arthur Rüegg and Lukas Felder, *40 Europäische Wohnikonen Neu Gesehen*, Zurich, gta Verlag, 2007, p.104.

3 Guided tour written notes supplied at Schloss Charlottenhof, Potsdam.

4 Klaus Jan Philipp, *Karl Friedrich Schinkel: Late Projects*, Stuttgart, Axel Menges, 2000, p.27.

5 Iain Boyd Whyte, 'Charlottenhof: The Prince, the Gardener, the Architect and the Writer', *Architectural History*, vol.43, 2000, pp 1–23.

6 Barry Bergdoll, *Karl Friedrich Schinkel: An Architect for Prussia*, New York, Rizzoli, 1994, p.148. The sculpted medallions of night and day reinforce the narrative.

7 Boyd Whyte, 'Charlottenhof', p.16.

8 In the same year the painter Phillip Otto Runge had published his three-dimensional colour studies, *Farbenkugel*, before his untimely death at the age of 33. Goethe was a German polymath who considered colour to be a factor of shadow, rather than of light, and was chiefly interested in our experience of colour phenomena. Although his observations were dismissed as contrary to scientific understanding, his focus on colour contrasts, and in particular the optical interaction of adjacent hues, are re-enforced in later works, notably by the chemist Michel Eugène Chevreul, and in the 20th century by Josef Albers in his *Interaction of Color*, 1963. See Fiona McLachlan, *Architectural Colour in the Professional Palette*, Abingdon, Routledge, 2012, p.177.

9 The influence of Schinkel on Bindesbøll was most evident in early designs for the museum. He revisited Schinkel's work in 1833, and an initial design had a colonnaded portico similar to the Altes Museum in Berlin (1830). However, while Schinkel placed colour in the recessed back wall of the south-facing Lustgarten facade, Bindesbøll revised his design to place the colour directly on the wall surfaces.

10 Bente Lange, *Thorvaldsen's Museum: Architecture – Colours – Light*, trans. Karen Steenhard, Copenhagen, The Danish Architectural Press, 2002, pp 23 and 57.

11 The adjoining houses were acquired and developed by Soane over an extended period between 1792 and 1824, and have recently been restored in a seven-year project by architects including Caruso St John. Patrick Baty, who is an expert on historical colour, was involved in the restorations.

12 Peter Thornton, 'Colour in Soane's House', in *Meddelelser fra Thorvaldsens Museum* [Communications from the Thorvaldsen's Museum], Copenhagen, Archivet, Thorvaldsens Museum 1989, pp 197–204, from Thorvaldsens Museum Archives, https://arkivet.thorvaldsensmuseum.dk/articles/colour-in-soanes-house, accessed 29 October 2021.

13 Lange, *Thorvaldsen's Museum*, p.89.

14   ibid., pp 64–5. Lange suggests that the architect waited until after the building committee had approved the plans before giving in to his 'passion for colour', clearly aware of the controversy it would cause.

15   Le Corbusier, 'Fresco', *L'Esprit Nouveau*, no.19, 1923, quoted in Romy Golan, *Muralnomad: The Paradox of Wall Painting, Europe 1927–1957*, New Haven, CT and London, Yale University Press, 2009, p.19.

16   Le Corbusier also infamously made a series of unsympathetic and gaudy murals inside Eileen Gray's E1027 house, which has been widely interpreted as a personally spiteful act. Gray's house is discussed in Chapter 5.

17   Jean-Louis Cohen with Staffan Ahrenberg, *Le Corbusier's Secret Laboratory: From Painting to Architecture*, Ostfildern, Hatje Cantz, 2013, p.135.

18   Arthur Rüegg (ed.), *Polychromie Architecturale: Les Claviers de Couleur de Le Corbusier de 1931 et de 1959*, Basel, Birkhäuser, 1998 (repr. 2006).

19   Maurice Raynal, *L'Esprit Nouveau*, issue 7, p.807, April 1921, quoted in Jan de Heer, *The Architectonic Colour: Polychromy in the Purist Architecture of Le Corbusier*, Rotterdam, 010 Publishers, 2009, p.60.

20   For example, in an installation at Blenheim Palace (2018) of Yves Klein's *Venus Bleue (S41) –* 1962/1982 IKB, International Klein Blue pigment and synthetic resin on plaster torsos – seen displayed against warm tones, the blue clearly appears to leap forward, as would a highly saturated red.

21   De Heer, *The Architectonic Colour*, pp 116–17. Original sketches by René Guiette/Fondation Le Corbusier, Paris.

22   For example, *Still Life of the Pavilion of L'Esprit Nouveau*, oil on canvas, 81 × 100 cm (31 ⅞ × 39 ⅜ in), 1924, Fondation Le Corbusier, Paris F.L.C.141, or *Still Life with a Siphon*, oil on canvas, 73 × 60 cm (28 ¾ × 23 ⅝ in), 1921, Fondation Le Corbusier, Paris F.L.C.139.

23   Wassily Kandinsky and Oskar Schlemmer led the painting course at the Bauhaus from 1922.

24   De Heer, *The Architectonic Colour*, p.149, suggests that Le Corbusier may have been drawing on the theory of Charles Blanc, *Grammaire des arts du dessin*, Paris, 1870. Blanc referred to architecture as first in terms of primacy, but also in time. Architecture, painting and colour had initially been bound together and only subsequently found independence.

25   Rüegg, *Polychromie Architecturale*, p.43.

26   Juan Serra, Jorge Llopis, Ana Torres and Manuel Giménez, 'Color Combination Criteria in Le Corbusier's Purist Architecture Based on Salubra *Claviers* from 1931', *Color Research and Application*, vol.41, no.1, February 2016, pp 85–100.

27   Opponent pigments – such as red and green, orange and blue, violet and yellow – offer a direct hue contrast. Goethe, Chevreul and, later, Johannes Itten, observed that a dynamic balance between hues is also dependent on the physical extent of the hue. For example, blue requires ⅔ of the area to ⅓ orange to achieve a visual balance. See McLachlan, *Architectural Colour in the Professional Palette*, pp 132–4.

28   De Heer, *The Architectonic Colour*, pp 119 and 132. It is noted, however, that this may have had more to do with the fact that Le Corbusier never visited the site or the building under construction and so the apparent ease with which one entirely different colour scheme could be supplanted may have less validity as an example.

29   Despite Le Corbusier's focus on colour combinations in the Salubra range, there is less evidence to suggest whether the optical interaction between hues was a specific aim of the 'promenade architecturale', as was evident in Lux Guyer's houses of the same period, such as her SAFFA House (1928), a prototype of which was originally built for the Schweizerische Ausstellung für Frauenarbeit (Swiss Exhibition for Women's Work) in Bern, after which it was relocated to Aarau and finally to a permanent place in Stäfa, on Lake Zurich.

30   Rüegg, *Polychromie Architecturale*, p.54 (letter, Le Corbusier to Marcel Levaillant, 26 February 1933, from Alger, Fondation Corbusier).

31   ibid., p.99.

32   'Peter Wilson and Mark Dorrian in Conversation', *Journal of Architecture*, vol.26, no.5, 2021, p.1.

33   See also Fiona McLachlan, 'Visual Heuristics for Colour Design', in Igea Troiani and Suzanne Ewing (eds) *Visual Research Methods in Architecture*, Bristol, Intellect, 2021, pp 335–52.

34   Peter Wilson, 'Small World Theory: An Exhibition by Peter Wilson in Berlin', Architektur Galerie, Berlin, 26 September–26 October 2019, https://bolles-wilson.com/news/25-09-19-small-world-theory-an-exhibition-by-peter-wilson-in-berlin/, accessed 16 July 2021.

35   Richard Sennett, *The Craftsman*, New Haven, CT, Yale University Press, 2008, p.ix.

36 A reference by Wilson to the renewed interest in hand drawings by a generation of architects who trained at the Architectural Association in the 1980s, now being documented by scholars and archived through the extensive Drawing Matter collection established by Niall Hobhouse. See *Indian Summer and Thereafter*, where Wilson makes reference to this period, https://www.world-architects.com/en/events/peter-wilson-indian-summer-and-thereafter, accessed 29 October 2021.

37 Peter Wilson, interview notes made for the author, December 2020.

38 'Bolles+Wilson – Master Plan of Korça's City Center', *Divisare*, 23 July 2009, https://divisare.com/projects/103255-bolles-wilson-master-plan-of-korca-s-city-center, accessed 29 October 2021.

39 McLachlan, *Architectural Colour in the Professional Palette*, pp 17–18.

40 Wilson elaborates the choice of blue as indicative of a 'blue bruise on the city', in reference to the illegal construction of the original building.

41 Peter Wilson, written notes provided in response to the author's interview questions, October 2020.

42 Camillo Sitte, *Der Städtebau nach seinen künstlerischen Grundsätzen* [City Building According to Artistic Fundamentals], Vienna, G. Prachner, 1889, trans. Charles Stewart, New York, Reinhold, 1945.

43 Peter Wilson, *Some Reasons for Travelling to Albania*, Zurich, About Books, 2019, p.332.

44 'Bolles+Wilson – Master Plan', 23 July 2009.

45 Peter Wilson, notes provided in response to author's interview questions, October 2020.

46 ibid.

47 ibid.

48 ibid.

4   PICTORIAL SPACE

1   The work required a major, two-month-long installation, plus 42 tons of steel, plasterboard and glass.

2   Roderick Lumsden, 'The Moving Oculus', in Ivana Wingham (ed.), *Mobility of the Line: Art, Architecture, Design*, Basel, Birkhäuser, 2013, p.183.

3   Julian Rose, *Sarah Oppenheimer in Perspective*, Mills College Art Museum, California, 2015, p.54.

4   John Kulvicki, 'Colour and the Arts: Chromatic Perspectives', in Derek Brown and Fiona Macpherson (eds), *The Routledge Handbook of Philosophy of Colour*, Abingdon, Routledge, 2021, pp 91–106.

5   Alberto Perez-Gomez, 'Sketching around *Lineamenta*', in Wingham, *Mobility of the Line*, p.28.

6   Maxwell Anderson, 'Pompeian Frescoes in the Metropolitan Museum of Art', *The Metropolitan Museum of Art Bulletin*, vol.45, no.3, Winter 1987–88, p.7.

7   The painting was installed as part of *Arthouses*, an annual festival where contemporary artists respond to an open call to make work within homes in Whitley Bay, initiated by the artist Tracy Tofield in 2010.

8   Catrin Huber, *Expanded Interiors at Herculaneum and Pompeii*, Bielefeld/Berlin, Kerber Verlag, 2019, pp 124–30.

9   Interview with the artist, April 2021. See also Catrin Huber, *Fictional Spaces*, Sunderland, Art Editions North, 2013.

10 John White, *The Birth and Rebirth of Pictorial Space*, London, Faber & Faber, 1957 (repr. 1987), p.263.

11 Hans Feibusch, *Mural Painting*, London, Adam and Charles Black, 1946, p.31.

12 ibid.

13 ibid., p.34.

14 Key works by these artists include – Victor Pasmore, *Metamorphosis* (1962), Renold Building, Manchester and the *Apollo Pavilion* (1963), Peterlee; Patrick Heron, *Orange and Lemon with White* and *Four Vermilions* (1965), University of Warwick; Sol LeWitt, wall drawings (1988), Bankers Trust Company, Dashwood House, City of London; Mark Rothko, Rothko Chapel (1964–1971), Houston; and Yves Klein, untitled, blue sponge reliefs (1959), Gelsenkirchen Musiktheater.

15 Clement Greenberg, *Art and Culture: Critical Essays*, London, Thames & Hudson, 1973, p.136.

16 We can see this optical oscillation very evidently in the later works of Bridget Riley where fugitive colours appear that do not exist on the surface of the painting. See Fiona McLachlan, *Architectural Colour in the Professional Palette*, Abingdon, Routledge, 2012, p.69.

17 Interview between Werner Ruhnau and François Perrin in Yves Klein, *Air Architecture, 1951–2004*, ed. Peter Noever and François Perrin, Los Angeles, MAK-Center for Art and Architecture/Ostfildern, Hatje Cantz, 2014, p.106.

18 ibid., p.40.

19 Gaston Bachelard, 'The Blue Sky', in *L'air et les songes: Essai sur l'imagination du mouvement* [Air and

Dreams: An Essay on the Imagination of Movement], Paris, Librarie José Corti, 1943 (repr. Dallas Institute Publications, 1988, pp 165 and 168.

20 Michael Schreyach, 'The Crisis of Jackson Pollock's *Mural* as a Painting', *Getty Research Journal*, no.9, supp.1, 2017, p.184.

21 ibid., p.187.

22 Gunnar Ekelöf is referenced by Dr Michael Tucker in his introduction to Ian McKeever, *In Praise of Painting: Three Essays*, Brighton, University of Brighton, 2005.

5   ETHEREAL MATERIAL

1   Including two further houses: Tempe à Pailla (1934) and Lou Perou (1958).

2   Rachel Siobhan Tyler, 'Revealing the Hidden Colour in Representations of Eileen Gray's Modern Architecture and Design', *Journal of Design History*, vol.33, no.2, May 2020, pp 123–39.

3   Beatriz Colomina, 'Battle Lines: E1027', in Diana Agrest, Patricia Conway and Leslie Jane Weisman, *The Sex of Architecture*, New York, Harry N. Abrams, 1996, pp 167–82.

4   Peter Adam and Andrew Lambirth, *Eileen Gray: The Private Painter*, London, Lund Humphries and Osbourne Samuel, 2015, p.15.

5   Examples of Eileen Gray's designs for carpets are included in Sonia Delaunay, *Tapis et Tissus*, Paris, Editions d'art Charles Moreau, c.1929, together with now-celebrated women Bauhaus weavers, Gunta Stölzl and Anni Albers.

6   Katrin Trautwein, *Farben für die Sinne: Eileen Gray und das Haus am Meer* [Colours for the Senses: Eileen Gray and the House by the Sea], Uster, kt.COLOR, 2017, p.8, https://www.ktcolor.ch/de/blog.aspx?nwsid=21, accessed 29 October 2021.

7   There has been outrage also in the way the house was subsequently overpainted by Le Corbusier, including the addition of his gaudy murals. For Gray, the colour design, materials, furniture and fittings were not only sufficient, but were the essence of the project as a harmonious composition, with no further embellishment needed. Gray was heartbroken and did not return until many years later, after World War II.

8   Rem Koolhaas (with Norman Foster and Alessandro Mendini), *Colours*, Blaricum, V+K Publishing, 2001, p.2.

9   Ludwig Wittgenstein, *Remarks on Colour*, 50c III-154, 1950, ed. G.E.M. Anscombe, trans. Linda L. McAlister and Margarete Schättle, Oxford, Blackwell Publishing, 1979. Wittgenstein also discusses more complex phenomena such as translucency, transparency and luminosity.

10   John Tuomey, *Architecture, Craft and Culture*, Dublin, Gandon, 2004, p.42.

11   Adrian Forty, *Concrete and Culture: A Material History*, London, Reaktion Books, 2012, p.44.

12   Jacob van der Beugel, 'Artwork: "Matter in Grey" Illustrates Progression of Alzheimer's', https://www.ch.cam.ac.uk/chemistry-of-health/artwork-matter-grey-illustrates-progression-alzheimers, accessed 29 October 2021.

13   The work is one of a series of artworks made as floor installations by Martin Creed. *Work No. 1347* (2012) was also with Haworth Tompkins for a restaurant in London, and *Work No. 1051* (2013) is now permanently installed as part of the collection at the Museo Jumex in Mexico City.

14   The client was Crispin Kelly, Peter Salter was the principal designer, with Fenella Collingridge as associate designer, artist Antoni Malinowski as colour consultant, and the executive architects were Mole Architects and John Comparelli Architects.

15   Jay Merrick, 'Squash-Luxe', *Architectural Review*, vol.241, no.1438, February 2017, p.41.

16   Will Hunter, 'Walmer Yard', *Architects' Journal*, vol.244, no.1, December 2017, p.30.

17   Peter Salter and Fenella Collingridge, *Drawing Walmer Yard*, London, Piano Nobile Publications, no.42, 2016.

18   The outer terracotta facades are also varied in colour, based on the architects' (Kohn Pedersen Fox Associates) contextual studies of earthen clay colours. The glass manufacturers were Scheuten Glas and BGT Bischoff Glastechnik GmbH. The client was the MTD Group, which was supportive of the collaboration.

19   The architects were PLP and the ceramic facade was itself a collaboration between three manufacturers: James & Taylor, based in England, translated the architect's colour palette into terracotta glazes; the glazed fins in 22 colour shades were then made in Bavaria, Germany by Moeding, with the artist working directly in the factory to apply the hand finish; the panels were made into units by GIG in Austria.

20 From an interview with the art commissioner for the project, Vivien Lovell, Modus Operandi, March 2021.

21 His collaborative work at the Laban Dance Centre with Herzog & de Meuron is discussed in Chapter 7.

22 George Blacklock, 'John Mitchell (1942–2014)', https://www.arts.ac.uk/about-ual/press-office/stories/john-mitchell-1942-2014, accessed 29 October 2021.

23 '3-2=1: Bridge, Bangle and Cornice with Richard Deacon and Eric Parry', https://www.ericparryarchitects.co.uk/meeting-architecture-richard-deacon-eric-parry/; and 'Saturated Space VIII: Eric Parry', http://www.saturatedspace.org/2016/11/saturated-space-viii-eric-parry.html, accessed 29 October 2021.

24 Fiona McLachlan and Beichen Yu, 'Vague Memories: Old Colour in the City: The Re-introduction of Copperas Render in Scotland', in Maria Godyń, Bożena Groborz and Agata Kwiatkowska-Lubańska (eds), Proceedings of the 2016 Colour-Culture-Science Conference, Jan Matejko Academy of Fine Arts in Krakow, Krakow, pp 205–13, CCS – Colour-Culture-Science Conference, Krakow, Poland, November 2016.

25 Some traditional pigments are also highly toxic, which rightly restricts their use. See also FionaMcLachlan, Architectural Colour in the Professional Palette, Abingdon, Routledge, 2012, pp 18–24.

26 His work with Haworth Tompkins is further discussed in Chapters 2 and 7.

27 See Philip Ball, Bright Earth: The Invention of Colour, London, Viking, 2001, or Victoria Finlay, Color: A Natural History of the Palette, New York, Random House, 2004.

28 Funding from the Royal Society for Arts (RSA) 'Art for Architecture' programme.

29 Vikki Heywood, quoted by Pamela Buxton, 'Pure Theatre', Blueprint, March 2000, p.45, https://antonimalinowski.co.uk/bibliography/blueprint-pure-theatre/, accessed 29 October 2021.

30 Antoni Malinowski and Peter Wilson with Michael Nyman, 'Luxor Letters', AA Files: The Journal of the Architectural Association School of Architecture, no.48, Winter 2002, London, The Architectural Association, p.23.

31 Antoni Malinowski, 'New Paintings' exhibition, Gimpel Fils Gallery, London, 13 April–22 May 2004, http://www.gimpelfils.com/pages/exhibitions/exhibition.php?exhid=30&subsec=1, accessed 29 October 2021.

32 Malinowski and Wilson with Nyman, 'Luxor Letters', pp 15–32.

33 ibid., p.17 (letter dated 4 February 2002).

34 ibid., p.25.

35 Antoni Malinowski, quoted on University of Oxford Mathematical Institute website, https://www.maths.ox.ac.uk/node/14442, accessed 29 October 2021.

36 Ian McKeever, In Praise of Painting: Three Essays, Brighton, University of Brighton, 2005, p.XVIII.

37 See Henri Neuendorf, 'Anish Kapoor Angers Artists', 16 February 2016, https://news.artnet.com/art-world/anish-kapoor-vantablack-exclusive-rights-436610, accessed 29 October 2021.

38 Mark D. Fairchild, Color Appearance Models, Rochester Institute of Technology & Society of Photographic Scientists Engineers, 3rd edn, Chichester, Wiley, 2013, p.94.

39 David Batchelor, The Luminous and the Grey, London, Reaktion Books, 2014, p.49.

40 Nilgün Camgöz, Cengiz Yener and Dilek Güvenç, 'Effects of Hue, Saturation and Brightness: Part 2: Attention', Color Research and Application, vol.29, no.1, February 2004, pp 20–28.

41 Eliasson's work, Yellow Fog, was originally created for a temporary installation in New York in 1998, and is now permanently sited in Vienna.

6 THE ARTIST'S PERSPECTIVE

1 Tess Jaray, from an interview with the author, April 2021.

2 Zena O'Connor, 'Tactical Urbanism: Colour Interventions with Purpose', Color Research and Application, vol.46, no.3, January 2021, pp 516–23.

3 Designed by the arts group Superflex in collaboration with Bjarke Ingels Group (BIG) architects and Topotek 1, a German landscape architecture firm.

4 Antoni Malinowski and Adam Nathaniel Furman set up the 'Saturated Space' colour research group at the Architectural Association in London in 2011. Italian designer practice Memphis was established in the 1980s, led by Ettore Sottsass.

5 The book Interaction of Color was written by Albers in 1963, long after his time teaching at the

Bauhaus (1923–33). He had succeeded Johannes Itten who had established methods of colour teaching while there (1919–22) and published his seminal text *The Art of Colour* (1961) much later in life.

6   For example, Hilary Dalke, Paul J. Littlefair, David L. Loe and Nilgün Camgöz, *Lighting and Colour for Hospital Design*, London, HMSO, 2004, or Ruth Brent Tofle, Benjamin Schwarz, So-Yeon Yoon and Andrea Max-Royale, *Color in Healthcare Environments*, San Francisco, Coalition for Health Environments Research (CHER), 2003.

7   See also Chapter 7 on the role of the commissioner.

8   Renovated in 2016 by architect Philippe Samyn.

9   Jean Guirand, *The Figure Field: Looking at George Meurant's Paintings*, Society for Gestalt Theory, Brussels, Didier Devillez Editeur, 1994, p.3, http://www.gestalttheory. net/cms/uploads/pdf/arts/visual%20arts/Guiraud1994FigureField.pdf, accessed 13 January 2021.

10   Toby Paterson, solo exhibition, *An Experiment for Total Environment*, Durham Art Gallery, Durham (with works by Victor Pasmore), 2012. The show made a series of artworks in response to Peterlee New Town.

11   *Cluster Relief (Dunfermline Remnant)*, 2017, is sited in the Dunfermline Carnegie Library and Galleries by Richard Murphy Architects.

12   Toby Paterson, quoted in Lynn McGarry, 'Art and Soul', *The Caledonian*, Issue 1, 2017, p.6.

13   Toby Paterson, interview with the author, February 2021.

14   See also 'Mark Titchner and Martin Clark in Conversation', in Martin Clark (ed.), *Mark Titchner: It is You*, exh.cat, Bristol, Arnolfini Gallery, 2006, pp 94–5.

15   A second, larger artwork was intended to be installed in the adjacent main concourse but was not implemented. See Tess Jaray and Charles Darwent, *Desire Lines: The Public Art of Tess Jaray*, London, Ridinghouse, 2016, p.11.

16   Richard Cork, 'From the Studio to the City 1984–88', in *Tess Jaray: Paintings and Drawings from the Eighties*, London, Serpentine Gallery, 1988, p.31.

17   Tess Jaray, *Painting: Mysteries and Confessions*, London, Royal Academy of Arts, 2012, p.87.

18   Tess Jaray, Alistair Warman and Jonathan Watts, 'Affinities: Extracts from an Interview', in Tess Jaray and Doro Globus, *The Art of Tess Jaray*, London/Nottingham, Ridinghouse/Djanogly Gallery, 2014, p.241.

19   See Richard Davey, 'St Mary's Church', in Jaray and Darwent, *Desire Lines*, p.82.

20   John Kulvicki, 'Colour and the Arts: Chromatic Perspectives', in Derek Brown and Fiona Macpherson, *The Routledge Handbook of Philosophy of Colour*, Abingdon, Routledge, 2021, p.95.

21   Johann Wolfgang von Goethe, *Theory of Colour*, trans. Charles Lock Eastlake, 1840, repr. Abingdon, Routledge, 2018, pp 29–33.

7   COLLABORATIVE PRACTICES

1   Mark Pimlott, 'Natural Antagonism: Notes on Colour or Architecture', in Edward Whittaker and Alex Landrum (eds), *Painting with Architecture in Mind*, Bath, Wunderkammer Press, 2012, p.30.

2   Ponti is quoted, acknowledging his difficulties in painting the murals, in Ugo La Pietra (ed.), *Gio Ponti*, New York, Rizzoli, 1996, p.124.

3   Ettore Sottsass was an architect and designer who also worked across disciplines and was the founder of the Memphis Group in the 1980s.

4   Oskar Schlemmer and Wassily Kandinsky, who became head of painting at the Bauhaus in 1922, both focused students' work on large-scale mural paintings. The integrated 'Basic Course' (Vorkurs) architecture curriculum developed by Johannes Itten in 1923 combined the study of textiles, colour, glass and other materials alongside nature and construction studies.

5   Sibyl Moholy-Nagy, *Carlos Villanueva and the Architecture of Venezuela*, London, Alec Tiranti Ltd, 1964, p.69.

6   ibid., p.97.

7   ibid., p.99.

8   The design team included the acoustic engineer Robert B. Newman, who employed two main tactics: first, 'complete silence' was established with careful insulation/sound absorption; second special reflectors made from bent plywood over steel frames were then suspended below the ceiling and were capable of adjustment.

9   Moholy-Nagy, *Carlos Villanueva and the Architecture of Venezuela*, p.94.

10   Colin St John Wilson, 'Reflections on the Relation of Painting to Architecture', London, London Magazine Ltd, vol.19, no.1, 1 April 1979, p.36. The Arts Council of Great Britain initiated its *Art in Public Spaces* policy in 1976/7, becoming the catalyst for

public arts officer posts in regional arts associations and local authorities.

11   Eugene Rosenberg, *Architect's Choice: Art in Architecture in Great Britain since 1945*, London, Thames & Hudson, 1992.

12   ibid., p.24.

13   Quotations by architect Steve Tompkins in conversation with the author, London, 2019.

14   ibid.

15   The original Leeds Playhouse was designed by the Appleton Partnership and completed in 1990. The original orientation was a response to a masterplan by Terry Farrell, which was not fully realised. The renovation involved a radical re-organisation of the interior layout to push through a linear foyer and make the building more permeable.

16   From an interview with architects Nicola Walls and Eamon McGarrigle of Page\Park, May 2021.

17   A further iteration of the artwork was made into a print edition so that visitors to the Printmakers building could also purchase the artwork.

18   Rachel Duckhouse subsequently applied for funding from Creative Scotland to continue the collaboration with Page\Park during the 2020–21 pandemic lockdown.

19   Deanna Petherbridge (ed.), *Art for Architecture: A Handbook on Commissioning*, London, HMSO (from research conducted by Peter Fink and Lesley Green – Art & Architecture Research Team – Dept of Environment), 1987, p.10.

20   ibid., p.3.

21   Richard Cork, in Rosenberg, *Architect's Choice*, p.32.

22   Vivien Lovell has been involved in commissioning art for architectural projects since the mid-1980s and has worked on large-scale projects in Birmingham and Cardiff Bay. In response to a major conference, *Art for Architecture* in 1982, and subsequent steering group recommendations, several UK local authorities implemented successful schemes, but often these are applied to private inward investments as a requirement of planning permission, and paradoxically, not for publicly funded projects. Crucially the UK government did not implement the policy. Lovell's report, *Reviewing the Case for One Percent for Art* (2007) for the Arts Council England, documents the history behind the advocacy and distils the proposal, but again this has not come to fruition. She continues to track the timeline for public

art funding and remains an advocate for a strategic approach.

23   Ann Magnusson is an art consultant and artistic director with Stockholm-based AM Public. From an interview with the author, March 2021. Morag Myerscough's work is discussed in Chapter 6.

24   Bruce McLean, interview with the author, September 2020.

25   *The Floor, The Fence, The Fireplace*, solo exhibition, Anthony d'Offay Gallery, London, March 1987. McLean's early work was often temporal, and he seems at ease with the impermanence of 'permanent'. Gemma Padley, 'Studio Visit: Bruce McLean', Interview, *Elephant*, 8 November 2017, quotes him as follows: 'I'm interested in the gesture and the action – the thing being there one minute and not the next. I'm not interested in making things that remain in space.' See https://elephant.art/studio-visit-bruce-mclean/, accessed 4 August 2021.

26   Mel Gooding, *Bruce McLean*, London, Phaidon, 1990, p.104.

27   Catherine Hürzeler, 'Collaboration with Artists, Interview with Jacques Herzog', https://www.herzogdemeuron.com/index/projects/writings/conversations/huerzeler.html, accessed 10 March 2021.

28   See Catherine Hürzeler, 'Herzog & de Meuron and Gerard Ritcher's Atlas', in Philip Ursprung (ed.), *Herzog & de Meuron: Natural History*, Montreal, Canadian Centre for Architecture/Lars Müller Publishers, 2002, pp 200–215.

29   ibid., p.214.

30   ibid., p.215.

31   In terms of the images, it is interesting to learn that his original intention was to choose a vocabulary of mundane objects and represent them to the audience, yet recently he has become aware that some of his collected objects – such as a cassette tape included at the Laban wall – have become esoteric, anachronistic relics unrecognisable to a young audience; see 'Senior Loeb Scholar Lecture: Michael Craig-Martin', 31 March 2015, Harvard School of Design, chaired by Professor Mohsen Mostafavi, https://www.youtube.com/watch?v=F7DqG7vCnOc, accessed 29 October 2021.

32   *Interior (Papillon Gallery Project) (Wall drawings)*, 1993–2012. In the installation, the walls of each room were painted in saturated red, yellow, blue and green. The artwork was purchased by the Pompidou Centre in 2012 and is noted as a significant

development of Craig-Martin's in-situ work. See https://www.centrepompidou.fr/en/ressources/oeuvre/c4rgErR, accessed 29 October 2021.

33 Jane Rendell, *Art and Architecture: A Place Between*, London/New York, I.B. Tauris & Co. Ltd, 2006, p.28.

8   CONSTRUCTING THE INSEPARABLE

1   Iain Boyd Whyte, 'Charlottenhof: The Prince, the Gardener, the Architect and the Writer', published text from the Annual Lecture of the Society of Architectural Historians of Great Britain, given at the Courtauld Institute, London, 1999, *Architectural History: Journal of the Society of Architectural Historians of Great Britain*, vol.43, 2000, pp 1–23.

2   Alain de Botton, from a lecture at the Architectural Association, London, October 2012, https://www.youtube.com/watch?v=HbaoXri6JBM, accessed 29 October 2021.

3   See Catherine Slessor, 'Taj on the Stour', *Architectural Review*, September 2015, pp 64–73. FAT Architecture was disbanded shortly after the project was completed, forming separate practices.

4   From an interview by Simon Hattenstone, 'Grayson Perry: Just because you don't have a dress on doesn't stop you being a Tranny', *The Guardian*, 8 October 2014, https://www.theguardian.com/artanddesign/2014/oct/04/grayson-perry-dress-tranny-art-who-are-you-tv, accessed 29 October 2021.

5   Steve Rose, 'The Making of *A House for Essex*', 2014, https://www.living-architecture.co.uk/the-houses/a-house-for-essex/architecture/, accessed 5 August 2021.

6   The use of colour by Soane has been a thread through several projects in this book, from architects such as Karl Friedrich Schinkel and Michael Gottlieb Bindesbøll, to artists Sinta Tantra and Catrin Huber who have made installations set in Soane's architectural projects at Dulwich and Pitzhanger respectively. See Chapters 3, 4 and 6.

9   REFLECTIONS ON ART IN ARCHITECTURE

1   Jane Rendell, *Art and Architecture: A Place Between*, London/New York, I.B. Tauris & Co. Ltd, 2006, p.4.

2   This is fully explored in Mark Wigley, *White Walls, Designer Dresses: The Fashioning of Modern Architecture*, Cambridge, MA, MIT, 1995; see also, Mark Pimlott, 'Natural Antagonism: Notes on Colour or Architecture', in Edward Whitaker and Alex Landrum (eds), *Painting with Architecture in Mind*, Bath, Wunderkammer Press, 2012, p.29.

3   Examples include muf architecture/art, and Assemble, which is now established as an agency for collaborative and co-working. Assemble won the UK's most prestigious award for art, the Turner Prize, in 2015, provoking a debate on the nature of art.

Bibliography

Adam, Peter and Andrew Lambirth, *Eileen Gray: The Private Painter*, London, Lund Humphries and Osbourne Samuel, 2015

Agrest, Diana, Patricia Conway and Leslie Jane Weisman, *The Sex of Architecture*, New York, Harry N. Abrams, 1996

Albers, Josef, *Interaction of Color*, New Haven, CT, Yale University Press, 1963; rev. edn, 2006

Alliez, Eric, and Jean-Claude Bonne, 'Matisse in the Becoming-Architecture of Painting', in Edward Whittaker and Alex Landrum (eds), *Painting with Architecture in Mind*, Bath, Wunderkammer Press and Bath School of Art and Design, 2012

Alpers, Svetlana and Michael Baxendall, *Tiepolo and the Pictorial Intelligence*, New Haven, CT and London, Yale University Press, 1994

Alsop, Will, Bruce McLean and Jan Störmer, *City of Objects: Designs on Berlin*, London, Architectural Press, 1992

Amato, Joseph, *Surfaces: A History*, Berkeley, CA and London, University of California Press, 2013

Anderson, Maxwell, 'Pompeian Frescoes in the Metropolitan Museum of Art', *The Metropolitan Museum of Art Bulletin*, vol.45, no.3, Winter 1987–8

Anter, Karen Fridell and Ulf Klarén, *Colour and Light: Spatial Experience*, New York, Routledge, 2017

Arnheim, Rudolf, *Art and Visual Perception: A Psychology of the Creative Eye*, Berkeley, CA, University of California Press, 1974

Bachelard, Gaston, *L'air et les songes: Essai sur l'imagination du mouvement* [Air and Dreams: An Essay on the Imagination of Movement], Paris, Librarie José Corti, 1943 (repr. Dallas Institute Publications, 1988)

Ball, Philip, *Bright Earth: The Invention of Colour*, London, Viking, 2001

Batchelor, David, *Chromophobia*, London, Reaktion Books, 2000

Batchelor, David, *The Luminous and the Grey*, London, Reaktion Books, 2014

Baty, Patrick, *The Anatomy of Colour*, New York, Thames & Hudson, 2017

Baudin, Katia (ed.), *Fernand Léger: Painting in Space*, Cologne, Museum Ludwig/Munich, Hirmer Verlag, 2016

Bergdoll, Barry, *Karl Friedrich Schinkel: An Architect for Prussia*, New York, Rizzoli, 1994

Birren, Faber, *Colour and Human Response*, New York, Van Nostrand Reinhold Co., 1978

Bird, Michael, 'Myth and Continuity: Peter Lanyon's Porthmeor', in *Porthmeor: A Peter Lanyon Mural Rediscovered*, Anthony Hepworth (curator), Victoria Art Gallery, Bath/North East Somerset Council, 2008

Blundell Jones, Peter and Mark Meagher (eds), *Architecture and Movement: The Dynamic Experience of Buildings and Landscapes*, Abingdon, Routledge, 2015

Borchardt-Hume, Achim (ed.), *Rothko: The Late Series*, London, Tate, 2008

Braham, William W., *Modern Color/Modern Architecture: Amédée Ozenfant and the Genealogy of Color in Modern Architecture*, Burlington, VT, Ashgate Pub. Co., 2002

Brown, Derek and Fiona Macpherson (eds), *The Routledge Handbook of Philosophy of Colour*, Abingdon, Routledge, 2021

Bruges, Jason, 'Architecture and Audience', in Manuel Kretzer and Ludger Hovestadt (eds), *Alive: Advancements in Adaptive Architecture*, Basel, Birkhäuser, 2014, pp 129–32

Bruno, Giuliana, *Surface: Matters of Aesthetics, Materiality, and Media*, Chicago, IL and London, University of Chicago Press, 2014

Buxton, Pamela, 'Pure Theatre', *Blueprint*, March 2000, pp 42–7

Cabeleira, João, 'Experiencing Architecture through Baroque Image: Gonçalves Sena, Painted Architecture as Architectural Space', *The International Journal of the Image*, vol.1, no.2, 2011, pp 119–34

Caivano, José Luis, 'Research on Color in Architecture and Environmental Design: Brief History, Current Developments, and Possible Future', *Color Research & Application*, vol.31, no.4, 2006, pp 350–63

Camgöz, Nilgün, Cengiz Yener and Dilek Güvenç, 'Effects of Hue, Saturation and Brightness: Part 2: Attention', *Color Research and Application*, vol.29, no.1, February 2004, pp 20–28

Canaday, John, *Metropolitan Seminars in Art: Portfolio 8, Techniques*, New York, Metropolitan Museum of Art, 1958

Caygill, Howard, *Walter Benjamin: The Colour of Experience*, London, Routledge, 1998

Chevreul, Michel Eugène, *The Laws of Contrast of Colour: and their application to the arts of painting, decoration of buildings, mosaic work, tapestry and carpet weavers, calico weaving, calico printing, dress, paper staining, printing*, trans. John Spanton, London, G. Routledge & Co., 1859

Clark, Martin (ed.), *Mark Titchner: It Is You*, exh.cat., Bristol, Arnolfini Gallery, 2006

Cohen, Jean-Louis with Staffen Ahrenberg, *Le Corbusier's Secret Laboratory: From Painting to Architecture*, Ostfildern, Hatje Cantz, 2013

Colomina, Beatriz, 'Battle Lines: E1027', in Diana Agrest, Patricia Conway and Leslie Jane Weisman (eds), *The Sex of Architecture*, New York, Harry N. Abrams, 1996, pp 167–82

Cork, Richard, 'From the Studio to the City 1984–88', in *Tess Jaray: Paintings and Drawings from the Eighties*, London, Serpentine Gallery, 1988

Craig-Martin, Michael, *Michael Craig-Martin: Ordinariness*, artwork © Michael Craig-Martin; Miriam Perez and PerryDuke, Gagosian Quarterly, London, 2019 [video], https://gagosian.com/quarterly/2019/08/12/michael-craig-martin-ordinariness-video, accessed 19 October 2021

Craig-Martin, Michael, 'Senior Loeb Scholar Lecture: Michael Craig-Martin', 31 March 2015, Harvard School of Design, chaired by Professor Mohsen Mostafavi [video], https://www.youtube.com/watch?v=F7DqG7vCnOc, accessed 12 September 2021

Creed, Martin, *Work No 1051*, Mexico City, photos by Moritz Bernoully, https://divisare.com/projects/392871-martin-creed-moritz-bernoully-work-no-1051, accessed 19 October 2021

Dalke, Hilary, Paul J. Littlefair, David L. Loe and Nilgün Camgöz, *Lighting and Colour for Hospital Design*, London, HMSO, 2004

Danés, Daniel, Mª José Pizarro, Joaquin Ibañez and Frank Marcano, 'University City of Caracas as a Colour Laboratory: Polychromie in the Work of Carlos Raúl Villanueva', *Revista Europea de Investigación en Arquitectura (REIA)*, no.17, pp 101–20

Darley, Gillian, 'Art and Craft: A House for Essex Stands as a Monument to an Imagination Run Wild', *The Architectural Review*, vol.240, no.1433, 2016, p.15

Davidts, Wouter, Susan Holden and Ashley Paine, *Trading between Architecture and Art: Strategies and Practices of Exchange*, Amsterdam, Valiz, 2019

De Botton, Alain, *The Architecture of Happiness*, London, Hamish Hamilton, 2006

De Botton, Alain, *Alain de Botton – Living Architecture* [video], Architectural Association, London, 28 October 2010, https://www.youtube.com/watch?v=HbaoXri6JBM, accessed 19 October 2021

De Heer, Jan, *The Architectonic Colour: Polychromy in the Purist Architecture of Le Corbusier*, Rotterdam, 010 Publishers, 2009

Delaunay, Sonia, *Tapis et Tissus*, Paris, Editions d'art Charles Moreau, c.1929

Doesburg, Theo van, *Principles of Neo-Plastic Art*, A Bauhaus Book, London, Lund Humphries, 1969

Dorrian, Mark (ed.), 'Architectural Lineaments – Adventures through the Work of Peter Wilson', *Journal of Architecture*, Special Issue, vol.26, no.5, 2021, pp 571–4

Droste, Magdalena, *Bauhaus, 1919–1933, Bauhaus-Archiv*, Cologne, Taschen, 2002

Düchting, Hajo, *Wassily Kandinsky 1866–1944: A Revolution in Painting*, Bonn, Benedict Taschen, 1996

Enright, M. (ed.), *Peter Lanyon: The Mural Studies*, London, Gimpel Fils Gallery, 1996

Fair, Alistair, *Play On: Contemporary Theatre Architecture in Britain*, London, Lund Humphries, 2019

Fairchild, Mark D., *Color Appearance Models*, Rochester Institute of Technology & Society of Photographic Scientists Engineers, 3rd edn, Chichester, Wiley, 2013

Fehr, Michael and Sanford Wurmfeld, Hunter College Art Gallery, *Seeing Red: On Non-objective Painting and Color Theory*, Cologne, Salon, 2004

Feibusch, Hans, *Mural Painting*, London, Adam and Charles Black, 1946

Finlay, Victoria, *Color: A Natural History of the Palette*, New York, Random House, 2004

Forty, Adrian, *Concrete and Culture: A Material History*, London, Reaktion Books, 2012

Foscari, Antonio, *Frescos within Palladio's Architecture: Malcontenta 1557–1575*, Zurich, Lars Müller Publishers, 2013

Gage, John, *Colour and Culture*, Berkeley, CA, University of California Press and London, Thames & Hudson, 1999

Geers, Kersten, Jelena Pančevac and Andrea Zanderigo (eds), *The Difficult Whole: A Reference Book on Robert Venturi, John Rauch and Denise Scott Brown*, Zurich, Park Books, 2016

Gibson, James J., An *Ecological Approach to Visual Perception*, New York, Houghton Mifflin, 1979, repr. New York, The Psychology Press, 2014

Goethe, Johan Wolfgang von, *Theory of Colour*, trans. Charles Lock Eastlake, 1840, repr. Abingdon, Routledge, 2018

Golan, Romy, *Muralnomad: The Paradox of Wall Painting*, *Europe 1927–1957*, New Haven, CT and London, Yale University Press, 2009

Gombrich, Ernst H., *Art and Illusion: A Study in the Psychology of Pictorial Representation*, 6th edn. London, Phaidon, 2002

Gooding, Mel, *Bruce McLean*, London, Phaidon, 1990

Gooding, Mel, *Abstract Art*, London, Tate Publishing, 2001

Gooding, Mel, *Kurt Schwitters*, London, Bernard Jacobsen Gallery, 2013

Greenberg, Clement, *Art and Culture: Critical Essays*, London, Thames & Hudson, 1973

Guirand, Jean, *The Figure-Field: Looking at George Meurant's Paintings*, Society for Gestalt Theory, Brussels, Didier Devillez Editeur, 1994, http://www.gestalttheory.net/cms/uploads/pdf/arts/visual%20arts/Guiraud1994FigureField.pdf, accessed 13 January 2021

Hardy, Adam, 'The Expression of Movement in Architecture', *The Journal of Architecture*, vol.16, no.4, 2011, pp 471–97

Hattenstone, Simon, 'Grayson Perry: Just because you don't have a dress on doesn't stop you being a Tranny', *The Guardian*, 8 October 2014, https://www.theguardian.com/artanddesign/2014/oct/04/grayson-perry-dress-tranny-art-who-are-you-tv, accessed 29 October 2021

Hirsch, Helen and Sarah Oppenheimer, *Invitation to a Reorientation in Space: N-01*, Kunstmuseum, Thun, Switzerland, Verlag für moderne Kunst, 2020, https://www.sarahoppenheimer.com/info/texts, accessed 20 October 2021

Hopkins, Owen and Erin McKellar (eds), 'Multi-form: Architecture in an Age of Transition', *Architectural Design Special Issue*, vol.91, no.1, January/February 2021

Huber, Catrin, *Fictional Spaces*, Sunderland, Art Editions North, 2013

Huber, Catrin, *Expanded Interiors at Herculaneum and Pompeii*, Bielefeld and Berlin, Kerber Verlag, 2019

Huber, Catrin, 'Expanded Interiors: Bringing Contemporary Site-Specific Fine-Art Practice to Roman Houses at Herculaneum and Pompeii', in Nick Cass, Gill Park and Anna Powell, *Contemporary Art in Heritage Spaces*, London and New York, Routledge, 2020

Hunter, Will, 'Walmer Yard', *Architects' Journal*, vol.244, no.1, December 2017

Hürzeler, Catherine, 'Collaboration with Artists, Interview with Jacques Herzog', https://www.herzogdemeuron.com/index/projects/writings/conversations/huerzeler.html, accessed 10 March 2021

Hürzeler, Catherine, 'Herzog & de Meuron and Gerhard Richter's Atlas', in Philip Ursprung (ed.), *Herzog & de Meuron: Natural History*, Montreal, Canadian Centre for Architecture and Lars Müller Publishers, 2002, pp 200–215

Itten, Johannes, *The Art of Color: The Subjective Experience and Objective Rationale of Color*, New York, Reinhold Publishing Co., 1961

Jaray, Tess, *Painting: Mysteries and Confessions*, London, Royal Academy of Arts, 2012

Jaray, Tess, Richard Cork and Robin Vousden, *Jess Jaray: Paintings and Drawings from the Eighties*, exh.cat., London, Serpentine Gallery, 1988

Jaray, Tess and Charles Darwent, *Desire Lines: The Public Art of Tess Jaray*, London, Ridinghouse, 2016

Jaray, Tess and Doro Globus, *The Art of Tess Jaray*, London and Nottingham, Ridinghouse and Djanogly Gallery, 2014

Joelson, Jo, *Library of Light: Encounters with Artists and Designers*, London, Lund Humphries, 2019

Johnston, Alan, *Tactile Geometry*, London, Bartha Contemporary, 2015

Kandinsky, Wassily, *Concerning the Spiritual in Art*, 1911, trans. Michael T.H. Sadler, repr. Las Vegas, IAP, 2009

Kane, Carolyn, 'Broken Colour in a Modern World: Chromatic Failures in Purist Art and Architecture', *Journal of the International Colour Association*, n.14, 2015, pp 1–13

Klein, Yves, *Air Architecture, 1951–2004*, ed. Peter Noever and François Perrin, Los Angeles, MAK-Center for Art and Architecture/Ostfilden, Hatje Cantz, 2014

Koolhaas, Rem (with Norman Foster and Alessandro Mendini), *Colours*, Blaricum, V+K Publishing, 2001

Kulvicki, John, 'Colour and the Arts: Chromatic Perspectives', in Derek Brown and Fiona Macpherson (eds), *The Routledge Handbook of Philosophy of Colour*, Abingdon, Routledge, 2021, pp 91–106

Kwinter, Sanford, *The Doors of Perception*, Sarah Oppenheimer, S-01, Annely Juda Fine Art, 2017, https://sarahoppenheimer.com/info/texts

La Pietra, Ugo (ed.), *Gio Ponti*, New York, Rizzoli, 1996

Lange, Bente, *Thorvaldsen's Museum: Architecture – Colours – Light*, trans. Karen Steenhard, Copenhagen, The Danish Architectural Press, 2002

Lanyon, Peter, Gimpel Fils (ed.), *Peter Lanyon: The Mural Studies*, London, Gimpel Fils Gallery, 1996

Leatherbarrow, David and Mohsen Mostafavi, *Surface Architecture*, Boston, MA, MIT Press, 2002

Le Corbusier, *The Decorative Art of Today*, Cambridge, MA, MIT Press, 1987

Léger, Fernand, *Functions of Painting,* trans. Alexandra Anderson, New York, Viking Press, 1973

Living Architecture, *Holidays in Modern Architecture: A House for Essex*, www.living-architecture.co.uk

Lønmo, Solveig (ed.), *Colour Space Motion through the Artwork of Edith Lundebrekke*, Norway, 2016

Loos, Adolf, *Ornament and Crime*, trans. Shaun Whiteside, London, Penguin Books, 2019

Lumsden, Roderick, 'The Moving Oculus', in Ivana Wingham (ed.), *Mobility of the Line: Art, Architecture, Design*, Basel, Birkhauser, 2013

Macpherson, Fiona, 'Novel Colour Experiences', in Derek Brown and Fiona Macpherson (eds), *The Routledge Handbook of Philosophy of Colour*, Abingdon, Routledge, 2021

Mahnke, Frank H. and Rudolf H. Mahnke, *Color and Light in Man-Made Environments*, New York, Van Nostrand Reinhold, 1987

Malinowski, Antoni and Peter Wilson with Michael Nyman, 'Luxor Letters', *AA Files: The Journal of the Architectural Association School of Architecture*, no.48, Winter 2002, pp 15–32

Mallgrave, Harry Francis, *From Object to Experience: The New Culture of Architectural Design*, New York, Bloomsbury

Martin, John Leslie, Ben Nicholson, and Naum Gabo, *Circle: International Survey of Constructive Art*, London, Faber & Faber, 1971

McGarry, Lynn, 'Art and Soul', *The Caledonian*, Issue 1, 2017

McKeever, Ian, *In Praise of Painting*, Brighton, University of Brighton, 2005

McLachlan, Fiona, *Architectural Colour in the Professional Palette*, Abingdon, Routledge, 2012

McLachlan, Fiona, 'Ethereal Material: Colour and Material Surface', *Proceedings of Institution of Civil Engineers: Construction Materials*, vol.166, no.6, 2013, pp 358–64

McLachlan, Fiona, 'Visual Heuristics for Colour Design', in Igea Troiani and Suzanne Ewing (eds), *Visual Research Methods in Architecture*, Bristol, Intellect, 2021, pp 335–52

McLachlan, Fiona and Ewen McLachlan, 'Colour and Contingency: Theory into Practice', *Architectural Theory Review*, vol.19, no.2, 2014, pp 243–58

McLachlan, Fiona and Beichen Yu, 'Vague Memories: Old Colour in the City: The Re-introduction of Copperas Render in Scotland', in Maria Godyń, Bożena Groborz and Agata Kwiatkowska-Lubańska (eds), *Proceedings of the 2016 Colour-Culture-Science Conference*, Jan Matejko Academy of Fine Arts in Krakow, Krakow, pp 205–13, CCS – Colour-Culture-Science Conference, Krakow, Poland, November 2016

McLachlan, Fiona, AnneMarie Neser, Lino Sibillano, Marcella Wenger-Di Gabriele and Stefanie Wettstein, *Colour Strategies in Architecture*, Basel, Schwabe Verlag in association with Haus der Farbe, 2015

McLean, Bruce, Mel Gooding and Bernard Jacobson Gallery, *Bruce McLean: The Shapes of Sculpture: An Exhibition of Recent Paintings*, exh.cat., London, Bernard Jacobson Gallery, 2012

Meerwein, Gerhard, Bettina Rodeck and Frank Mahnke, *Color: Communication in Architectural Space*, Basel, Birkhäuser, 2007

Merrick, Jay, 'Squash-Luxe', *Architectural Review*, vol.241, no.1438, February 2017, pp 40–44

Miller, Mary C., *Color for Interior Architecture*, New York and London, John Wiley and Sons, 1997

Moholy-Nagy, Sibyl, *Carlos Villanueva and the Architecture of Venezuela*, London, Alec Tiranti Ltd, 1964

O'Connor, Zena, 'Colour Harmony Revisited', *Color Research and Application*, vol.35, no.4, 2010, pp 267–73

O'Connor, Zena, 'Tactical Urbanism: Colour Interventions with Purpose', *Color Research and Application*, vol.46, no.3, 2021, pp 516–23

Oppenheimer, Sarah, 'Projects N 01', Kunstmuseum, Thun, Switzerland, 2020, https://sarahoppenheimer.com/projects/N-01

Ozenfant, Amédée, 'Colour: Experiments, Rules, Facts', *Architectural Review*, no.81, April 1937

Padley, Gemma, 'Studio Visit: Bruce McLean', Interview, *Elephant*, 8 November 2017, https://elephant.art/studio-visit-bruce-mclean/, accessed 4 August 2021

Pallasmaa, Juhani, 'Hapticity and Time: Notes on Fragile Architecture', *Architectural Review*, vol.207, no.1239, May 2000, pp 78–83

Pallasmaa, Juhani and Peter MacKeith (eds), *Encounters: Architectural Essays*, Helsinki, Rakennustieto, 2012

Parry, Eric, 'Eric Parry' [video], London, Architectural Association/Saturated Space VIII, 2016, http://www.saturatedspace.org/2016/, accessed 19 October 2021

Paterson, Toby and Judith Winter (eds), *Toby Paterson: Thresholds*, Maggie's Centres, Edinburgh Sculpture Workshop, 2015

Perez-Gomez, Alberto, 'Sketching around Lineamenta', in Ivana Wingham (ed.), *Mobility of the Line: Art, Architecture*, Design, Basel, Birkhauser, 2013

Petherbridge, Deanna, Peter Fink, Lesley Green and Great Britain, Department of the Environment, *Art for Architecture: A Handbook on Commissioning*, London, HMSO, 1987

Philipp, Klaus J., *Karl Friedrich Schinkel: Late Projects*, Stuttgart, Axel Menges, 2000

Pimlott, Mark, 'Natural Antagonism: Notes on Colour or Architecture', in Edward Whittaker and Alex Landrum (eds), *Painting with Architecture in Mind*, Bath, Wunderkammer Press/Bath School of Art and Design, 2012, pp 22–37

Pimlott, Mark, 'Blinky Palermo: Drawing and Painting on Walls', London, Architectural Association and Saturated Space, 2015, http://www.saturatedspace.org/2015/05/blinky-palermos-wall-drawings-wall.html, accessed 19 October 2021

Ponti, Gio and Ugo La Pietra, *Gio Ponti*, New York, Rizzoli, 1996

Ponti, Lisa L., *Gio Ponti: The Complete Work, 1923–1978*, Cambridge, MA, MIT Press, 1990

Porter, Tom, *Will Alsop – The Noise*, Abingdon, Routledge, 2011

Pye, Elizabeth, 'Wall Painting in the Roman Empire: Colour, Design and Technology', *Archaeology International*, vol.4, no.24, 2000, pp 24–7

Read, Herbert, *The Meaning of Art*, New York, Pitman Pub. Corp., 1951

Rendell, Jane, *Art and Architecture: A Place Between*, London/New York, I.B. Tauris & Co. Ltd, 2006

Risselada, Max (ed.), *Raumplan versus Plan Libre: Adolf Loos and Le Corbusier 1919–1930*, New York, Rizzoli, 1988

Rose, Julian, *Sarah Oppenheimer in Perspective*, Mills College Art Museum, California, 2015, pp 29–54, https://www.filepicker.io/api/file/OzgAmmIsQrCtcuiQBwSH

Rose, Steve, 'The Making of *A House for Essex*', 2014, https://www.living-architecture.co.uk/the-houses/a-house-for-essex/architecture/, accessed 5 August 2021

Rosenberg, Eugene, *Architect's Choice: Art in Architecture in Great Britain since 1945*, London, Thames & Hudson, 1992

Ross, Helen E., *Behaviour and Perception in Strange Environments*, London, Allen & Unwin, 1974

Rothko, Christopher, *Mark Rothko: From the Inside Out*, New Haven, CT, Yale University Press, 2015

Royal Society of Arts (Great Britain), *RSA Art for Architecture Award Scheme: Notes on Collaboration*, RSA Art for Architecture Award Scheme, 1999

Rüegg, Arthur (ed.), *Polychromie Architecturale: Les Claviers de Couleur de Le Corbusier de 1931 et de 1959*, Basel, Birkhäuser, 1998 (repr. 2006)

Rüegg, Arthur and Lukas Felder, *40 Europäische Wohnikonen Neu Gesehen*, Zurich, gta Verlag, 2007

Salter, Peter, Peter Beardsell, Mark Dorrian, Crispin Kelly, Fenella Collingridge and Matthew Ritchie, *Peter Salter: Walmer Yard*, London, Circa Press, 2019

Salter, Peter and Fenella Collingridge, *Drawing Walmer Yard*, London, Piano Nobile Publications, no.42, 2016

Sauerbruch, Matthias and Louisa Hutton (eds), *Sauerbruch Hutton: Colour in Architecture*, Berlin, Distanz, 2012

Schönemann, Heinz, *Karl Friedrich Schinkel Charlottenhof, Potsdam-Sanssouci*, Stuttgart/London, Axel Menges, 1997

Schreyach, Michael, 'The Crisis of Jackson Pollock's *Mural* as a Painting', *Getty Research Journal*, no.9, suppl.1, 2017, pp 183–99

Sennett, Richard, *The Craftsman*, New Haven, CT, Yale University Press, 2008

Serra, Juan, Jorge Llopis, Ana Torres and Manuel Giménez, 'Color Combination Criteria in Le Corbusier's Purist Architecture Based on Salubra Claviers from 1931', *Color Research and Application*, vol.41, no.1, February 2016, pp 85–100

Serrazanetti, Francesca and Matteo Schubert (eds), *Bolles+Wilson: Inspiration and Process in Architecture*, Milan, Moleskine srl, 2011

Simmonds, Rachel, 'The King's Theatre', *The Magazine of the Architectural Heritage Society of Scotland*, Autumn 2013, pp 24–7

Sitte, Camillo, *Der Städtebau nach seinen künstlerischen Grundsätzen* [City Building According to Artistic Fundamentals], Vienna, G. Prachner, 1889, trans. Charles Stewart, New York, Reinhold, 1945

Slessor, Catherine, 'Taj on the Stour', *Architectural Review*, September 2015, pp 64–73

Snodin, Michael, *Karl Friedrich Schinkel: A Universal Man*, New Haven, CT, and London, Yale University Press in association with the Victoria and Albert Museum, 1991

Sottsass, Ettore, *Notes on Colour*, ed. Barbara Radice, Italy, Abet Edizioni, 1993

St John Wilson, Colin, 'Reflections on the Relation of Painting to Architecture', London, London Magazine Ltd, vol.19, no.1, 1 April 1979

Swirnoff, Lois, *Dimensional Color*, New York, W.W. Norton & Co., 2003

Thornton, Peter, 'Colour in Soane's House', in *Meddelelser fra Thorvaldsens Museum* (Communications from the Thorvaldsen's Museum), Copenhagen, Archivet, Thorvaldsens Museum, 1989, pp 197–204

Tofle, Ruth Brent, Benjamin Schwarz, So-Yeon Yoon and Andrea Max-Royale, *Color in Healthcare Environments*, San Francisco, Coalition for Health Environments Research (CHER), 2003

Trautwein, Katrin, *Farben für die Sinne: Eileen Gray und das Haus am Meer* [Colours for the Senses and the House by the Sea], Uster, kt.COLOR, 2017

Troiani, Igea and Suzanne Ewing, *Visual Research Methods in Architecture*, Bristol, Intellect, 2021

Tuomey, John, *Architecture, Craft and Culture*, Dublin, Gandon, 2004

Tyler, Rachel Siobhan, 'Revealing the Hidden Colour in Representations of Eileen Gray's Modern Architecture and Design', *Journal of Design History*, vol.33, no.2, May 2020, pp 123–39

Ursprung, Philip (ed.), *Herzog & de Meuron: Natural History*, exh.cat., Canadian Centre for Architecture, Lars Müller, 2002

Venturi, Robert and Museum of Modern Art, New York, *Complexity and Contradiction in Architecture*, 2nd edn, Architectural Press, 1977

Villanueva, Paulina and Macia Pinto, *Carlos Raúl Villanueva*, Basel, Birkhäuser, 2000

Westerdahl, Eduardo, *Willi Baumeister*, Santa Cruz de Tenerife, Ediciones Gaceta de Arte, 1934

White, John, *The Birth and Rebirth of Pictorial Space*, London, Faber & Faber, 1957 (repr. 1987)

Whyte, Iain Boyd, 'Charlottenhof: The Prince, the Gardener, the Architect and the Writer', Annual Lecture of the Society of Architectural Historians of Great Britain, given at the Courtauld Institute, 1999, *Architectural History: Journal of the Society of Architectural Historians of Great Britain*, vol.43, 2000, pp 1–23

Whittaker, Edward and Alex Landrum (eds), *Painting with Architecture in Mind*, Bath, Wunderkammer Press and Bath School of Art and Design, 2012

Wigley, Mark, *White Walls, Designer Dresses: The Fashioning of Modern Architecture*, Cambridge, MA, MIT Press, 1995

Wilson, Peter, *Some Reasons for Travelling to Albania*, Zurich, About Books, 2019

Wilson, Peter, 'Peter Wilson and Mark Dorrian in Conversation', *Journal of Architecture*, vol.26, no.5, 2021

Wingham, Ivana (ed.), *Mobility of the Line: Art, Architecture, Design*, Basel, Birkhäuser, 2013

Wittgenstein, Ludwig, *Remarks on Colour*, ed. G.E.M. Anscombe, trans. Linda L. McAlister and Margarete Schättle, Oxford, Blackwell Publishing, 1979

Yendle, Brad, 'Visiting a Retrospective on Bruce McLean', *Architects' Journal*, 19 July 2014, n.p.

Zaugg, Rémy, *Architecture by Herzog & De Meuron, Wall Painting by Rémy Zaugg: A Work for Roche Basel*, Basel, Boston/Berlin, Birkhäuser, 2001

Zuidervaart, Lambert, *Adorno's Aesthetic Theory: The Redemption of Illusion*, Studies in Contemporary German Social Thought, Cambridge, MA, MIT Press, 1991

Index

Note: *italic* page numbers indicate figures.

Illustration Credits

The reproduction of the drawings and photographs listed below by figure number is courtesy of the following copyright holders:

0.1 Artist: Derek Roberts, Photo: Woolver; 0.2, 0.3 Photos: Woolver; 1.1 Photo: Woolver; 2.1 Hemis/Alamy Stock Photo; 2.2 Photo: © RMN-Grand Palais (Musée Fernand Léger)/ Adrien Didierjean, © ADAGP, Paris and DACS, London 2021; 2.3 Photo: Alan Johnston; 2.4 DI016544 Treppenhaus, Blick Richtung Süden vom Umkehrpodest aus, R. 3, Würzburg, Residenz und Hofgarten © Bildarchiv Foto Marburg/ Bayerische Schlösserverwaltung/Achim Bunz (CbDD); 2.5, 2.6 courtesy of John Byrne, Photos: Ron O'Donnell; 2.7 Research and Cultural Collections, University of Birmingham, © Estate of Peter Lanyon. All rights reserved, DACS 2021; 2.8 Photo: Matthias Schaller with permission from Professor A. Foscari; 2.9 Photo: Sigi Koezle; 2.10 Wikimedia Commons: Jean-Pierre Dalbérra, 2016, © DACS 2021; 2.11 Author, Theo van Doesburg, Alamy Stock Photo; 2.12 Photo: Fiona McLachlan; 2.13 Photo: Margherita Spiluttini © Architekturzentrum Wien, Collection; 2.14, 2.15 Photos: Felice Varini; 2.16 Photo: Fiona McLachlan; 2.17 Photo: Philip Vile, courtesy Haworth Tompkins; 2.18 Photo: Philip Vile, courtesy Haworth Tompkins; 2.19 Photo: Fiona McLachlan; 2.20 Photo: Philip Vile, courtesy Haworth Tompkins; 3.1 Winckelman u. Söhne, Berlin 1843, reproduction picture postcard, Staatliche Schlösser und Gärten, Berlin; 3.2, 3.3, 3.4, 3.5, 3.6, 3.7, 3.8, 3.9, 3.10, 3.11, 3.12, 3.13, 3.14 Photos: Fiona McLachlan; 3.15 UNESCO World Heritage Photo: Oliver Martin-Gambier © F.L.C./ADAGP; 3.16 © F.L.C./ ADGAP, Paris and DACS, London, 2021, Photo: Jean-Pierre Dalbéra, Wikimedia Commons; 3.17 © F.L.C./ADAGP, Paris and DACS, London 2021; 3.18, 3.19 © F.L.C./ADAGP, Paris and DACS, London 2021; 3.20 Photo: Cemal Emden, 2015; 3.21, 3.22 Images courtesy Architekturbüro Bolles Wilson © BOLLES+WILSON; 3.23 Image courtesy Architekturbüro Bolles Wilson © Roman Mensing; 3.24, 3.25 Images courtesy Architekturbüro Bolles Wilson © BOLLES+WILSON; 3.26, 3.27, 3.28 Images courtesy Architekturbüro Bolles Wilson © Roman Mensing; 3.29, 3.30, 3.31 Images courtesy Architekturbüro Bolles Wilson © BOLLES+WILSON; 4.1 Photo: Woolver; 4.2, 4.3 © Sarah Oppenheimer. Photos: Tom Little; 4.4 Image donated to Wikimedia Commons by Metropolitan Museum of Art; 4.5 Photo: Colin Davidson, courtesy Catrin Huber; 4.6 Photo: Michael Franke, courtesy Catrin Huber; 4.7 Photo: Amedeo Benestante, upon authorisation of the Ministry for Cultural Heritage and Environment, Pompeii; 4.8 Photo: Dietrich Hackenberg © Succession Yves Klein c/o ADAGP, Paris and DACS, London 2021; 4.9 © Succession Yves Klein c/o ADAGP, Paris and DACS, London 2021 Donation 1967 from The Friends of Moderna Museet, Photo: Woolver; 5.1 Collection Peter Adam; 5.2 Photo: kt.COLOR; 5.3 Photo: Fiona McLachlan; 5.4, 5.5 Photos: Paul Riddle; 5.6, 5.7, 5.8 Photos: Fiona McLachlan; 5.9 Image courtesy of the artist; 5.10, 5.11, 5.12 Photo: Fiona McLachlan; 5.13 Photo: Woolver; 5.14 Photo: © Stig Evans; 5.15 Photo: Woolver; 5.16 Photo: courtesy Royce Wood Studio; 5.17 Photo: Fiona McLachlan; 5.18, 5.19, 5.20, 5.21 Photos: Woolver; 5.22 Photo: Andy Chopping; 5.23 Photo: Valerie Bennett; 5.24 Image courtesy Architekturbüro Bolles Wilson © Christian Richters; 5.25 Photo: John Riddy; 5.26, 5.27 Photos: Valerie Bennett; 5.28 Photo: Fiona McLachlan; 5.29 Photo: Woolver; 5.30 Photo: Max McLachlan; 6.1 © Tess Jaray; 6.2 Photo: Woolver; 6.3, 6.4, 6.5 Sinta Tantra/Photo: Luca Piffaretti; 6.6 Photo: Jill Tate, courtesy Artfelt, Sheffield; 6.7, 6.8 Photos: Woolver; 6.9 Photo: Kajsa Juslin, courtesy AM Public, Stockholm; 6.10 Photo: Fiona McLachlan; 6.11 courtesy of The Artist and The Modern Institute/Toby Webster Ltd, Glasgow. Photo: Gilmar Ribeiro; 6.12 courtesy of The Artist and The Modern Institute/Toby Webster Ltd, Glasgow. Photo: Jamie Woodley; 6.13, 6.14 courtesy of The Artist and The Modern Institute/Toby Webster Ltd, Glasgow. Photo: Neale Smith; 6.15 Mark Titchner and the BUILDHOLLYWOOD family of JACK, JACK ARTS and DIABOLICAL for Your Space Or Mine; 6.16 Mark Titchner/Photo: Woolver; 6.17, 6.18 Mark Titchner/Photo: Fiona McLachlan; 6.19 Tess Jaray/Photo: Richard Bryant; 6.20, 6.21 Tess Jaray/Photos: Martine Hamilton Knight; 6.22 Tess Jaray/Photo: Woolver; 6.23, 6.24, 6.25 Photos: James Medcraft, Artwork: Jason Bruges Studio; 7.1 Photo: Carlo Calore in Abitare n. 550, courtesy Abitare; 7.2 Photo: courtesy Hotel Parco dei Principi; 7.3 Fundación Villanueva/Ricardo Armas; 7.4 © 2022 Calder Foundation, New York/DACS, London/Fundación Villanueva. Photo: Paolo Gasparini; 7.5 Photo: Hélène Binet; 7.6 Photo: Fiona McLachlan; 7.7 Photo: Jim Stephenson; 7.8, 7.9 Photos: Woolver; 7.10 Photo: Peter Cook; 7.11 Bruce McLean/ Photo: courtesy of the artist; 7.12, 7.13, 7.14 Photos: Fiona McLachlan; 8.1, 8.2 Photo: © Jack Hobhouse, courtesy Living Architecture; 8.3 Photo: Woolver; 8.4, 8.5 Photos: Simon-Fowler.com; 8.6, 8.7 Photo: © Jack Hobhouse, courtesy Living Architecture; 9.1 © Mark Bradford, courtesy the artist and Hauser & Wirth